P9-BBP-629

Advanced
Origami

FIREFLY BOOKS

A FIREFLY BOOK

Published by Firefly Books Ltd. 2000
Copyright © Dessain & Tolra/HER 2000

All rights reserved. No part of this publication may be reproduced, stored in a retrieval system or transmitted in any form or by any means, electronic, mechanical, photocopying, recording or otherwise, without the prior written permission of the publisher.

Second Printing, 2005

Publisher Cataloging-in-Publication Data (U.S.)
Boursin, Didier.
    Advanced origami : more than 60 fascinating and challenging projects for the serious folder / Didier Boursin ; translated by Ann Woollcombe.
(144) p. : ill. (some col.) ; cm.
Simultaneously published in France: Dessain et Tolra/HER 2000, "Le Livre de l'origami : pliages à vivre et à jouer."
Summary: 60+ projects to make a variety of origami models.
ISBN 1-55209-527-4
1. Origami. 2. Paper work. 3. Box making.
I. Title.
736.982-dc21   2000   CIP

Library and Archives Canada Cataloguing in Publication
Boursin, Didier.
    Advanced origami : more than 60 fascinating and challenging projects for the serious folder
Translation of: Le Livre de l'origami : pliages à vivre et à jouer
ISBN 1-55209-527-4

1. Origami.   I. Title
TT870.B6813 2000   736'.982   C99-932937-5

Published in the United States by
Firefly Books (U.S.) Inc.
P.O. Box 1338, Ellicott Station
Buffalo, New York 14205

Published in Canada by
Firefly Books Ltd.
66 Leek Crescent,
Richmond Hill, Ontario L4B 1H1

Cover design: Jacqueline Hope Raynor
Interior design and photo styling: Didier Boursin
Photography: Cactus Studio
Consultant: John Reid

Printed in France

Acknowledgements

I wish to thank all those who, from near and far, have encouraged me to create this book: my three children, Nina and Angelo, who have shared much of their creativity, and Tessa for her advice. Setsuko, my partner. Friends and designers, for their support and encouragement: L. Canovi, D. Brill, S. and M. Biddle, S. and Y. Momotani, J. Cunliff, T. Inoué, P. Jackson, S. Weiss, and K. Kasahara. Fabrice Besse, for his magnificent light-filled photographs. And all who appreciate my work and invite me to show it.
    You may write to me to share your experiences and discoveries:
    Didier Boursin
    Boutique Setsuko et Didier
    17, rue Sainte-Croix-de-la-Bretonnerie 75004 Paris

Contents

*	very easy
**	easy
***	difficult

The history of paper folding is probably as old as paper itself, and likely originated in China. Then, several centuries later in Japan, origami developed as a ceremonial art form within the Shinto tradition.

Originally a form of artistic expression, origami soon became a practical art form. Boxes were created to hold small offerings. Zigzag folds made from white paper held spices and medicines, and could be used to wrap small objects such as combs, fans, and hairpins.

As paper became a more accessible commodity, origami became something of a hobby. In France under Henry IV, napkin folding was an important aspect of ceremonial dinners, and the art developed a following among the courts of Europe. We know that Leonardo da Vinci used folding to study geometry and aerodynamics.

Today, children and adults the world over enjoy the ancient art of paper folding. Modern creators have passed on the tradition and enriched it with their own folds. Professionals such as architects and engineers use folding to help them develop new structures. Mathematicians use it to study geometry, teachers use it as an educational tool, and occupational therapists use it for the rehabilitation of hands and fingers.

In this book I present my own and my friends' creations: boxes to use for various occasions; invitation cards to announce your parties; airplanes that perform with precision and speed; decorative animals; and numerous other folds that will turn to magic in your hands.

Folds and Symbols

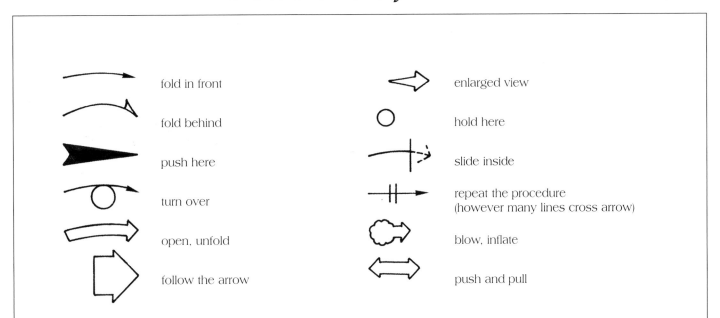

fold in front

fold behind

push here

turn over

open, unfold

follow the arrow

enlarged view

hold here

slide inside

repeat the procedure
(however many lines cross arrow)

blow, inflate

push and pull

valley fold

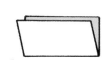

Fold a sheet of paper in half from the bottom.

You have a valley fold.

mountain fold

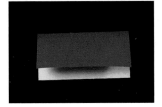

Fold a sheet of paper in half from the top.

You have a mountain fold.

crease

Note the difference between folding the paper and creasing (sometimes called marking the fold). When folding the paper (left square), the paper remains folded. When creasing the paper (right square), you unfold.

cut

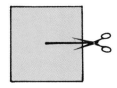

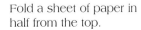

Make a cut as indicated whenever you see the scissors symbol.

pleat fold

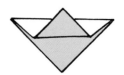

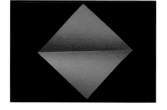

Fold a square of paper in half from the front.

You have a triangle.

Bring up one point.

Fold again as shown. You have a pleat fold.

matching the dots

Fold a sheet of paper from the front, as shown.

You have a valley fold.

equilateral triangle

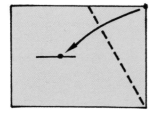
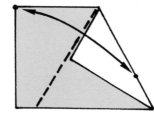
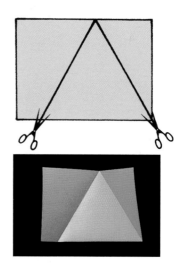

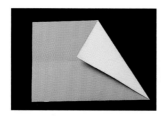

Starting with a rectangular sheet of paper, crease the center line, then bring the upper-right corner down to meet the center line.

Crease the left side as shown.

Unfold and you have a perfect equilateral triangle.

inside reverse fold

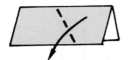

Make a valley fold, then bring the upper-right corner over as shown.

Then open.

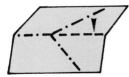 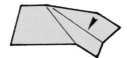

Push down in the center to make the center fold a valley fold. Make mountain folds on either side of the center fold. Then push in the right side.

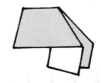

You have an inside reverse fold.

outside reverse fold

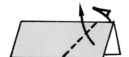

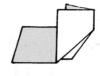

Make a valley fold, then bring the lower-right corner over as shown.

Then open.

Make the center fold a valley fold. Make mountain folds on either side of the center fold. Then push in the left side.

You have an outside reverse fold.

preliminary base

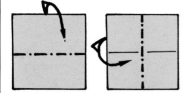    

On a square sheet of paper, crease a central mountain fold.

Then crease a second central mountain fold as shown.

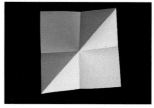

Crease a diagonal valley fold.

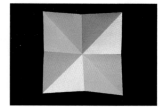

Then crease a second diagonal valley fold as shown.

Press on the center from behind.

Grasp two opposite corners, and bring the folds together to form a diamond shape.

Flatten the entire model.

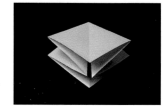

You have the preliminary base.

water-bomb base

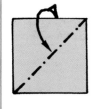 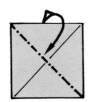   

On a square sheet of paper, crease a diagonal mountain fold.

Then crease a second diagonal mountain fold as shown.

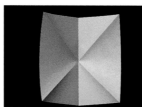

Crease a central fold in a valley fold.

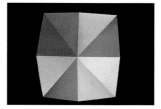

Then crease a second central valley fold.

Press on the center from behind.

Grasp two opposite corners, and bring the folds together to form a triangle.

Then flatten the entire model. You have the water-bomb base.

bird base

   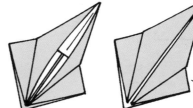 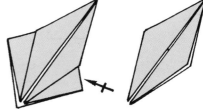

Make a preliminary base, then fold the edges to the central fold.

Fold down the upper triangle.

After unfolding the three points, grasp the bottom point of the first layer.

Bring up the bottom point inside the folds.

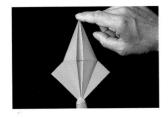   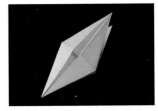

Flatten the entire fold.

Turn over and repeat the above steps.

After unfolding the sides, bring up the point inside the folds.

You have the bird base.

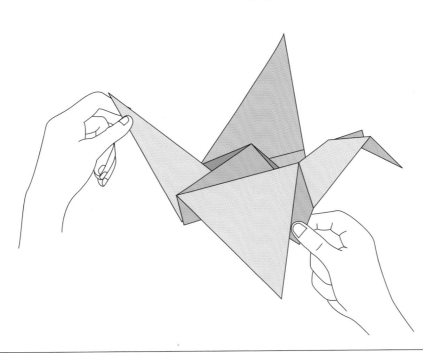

Boxes and Containers

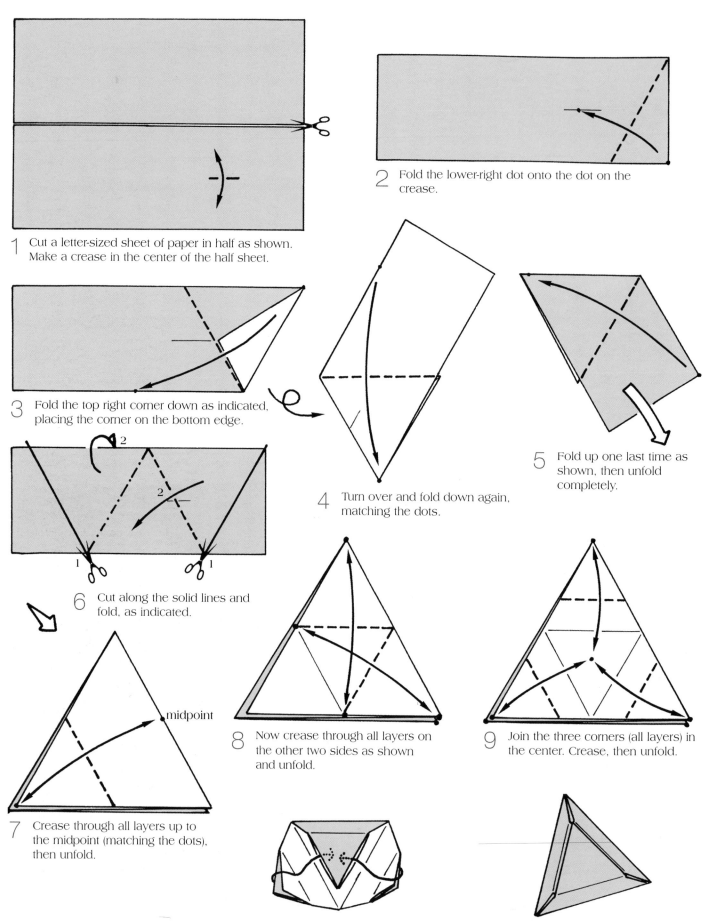

1 Cut a letter-sized sheet of paper in half as shown. Make a crease in the center of the half sheet.

2 Fold the lower-right dot onto the dot on the crease.

3 Fold the top right corner down as indicated, placing the corner on the bottom edge.

4 Turn over and fold down again, matching the dots.

5 Fold up one last time as shown, then unfold completely.

6 Cut along the solid lines and fold, as indicated.

7 Crease through all layers up to the midpoint (matching the dots), then unfold.

midpoint

8 Now crease through all layers on the other two sides as shown and unfold.

9 Join the three corners (all layers) in the center. Crease, then unfold.

10 The upper triangle is now folded back and made 3-dimensional. Slip the other two points into the pockets to close the box.

Triangular Box

JEWEL BOX. The most beautiful wrappings are those you create yourself, and the best gifts come in small packages. With a little folding, a simple sheet of paper is transformed into a lovely gift box that holds a favorite piece of jewelry.

For folds and symbols, see pages 5-9.

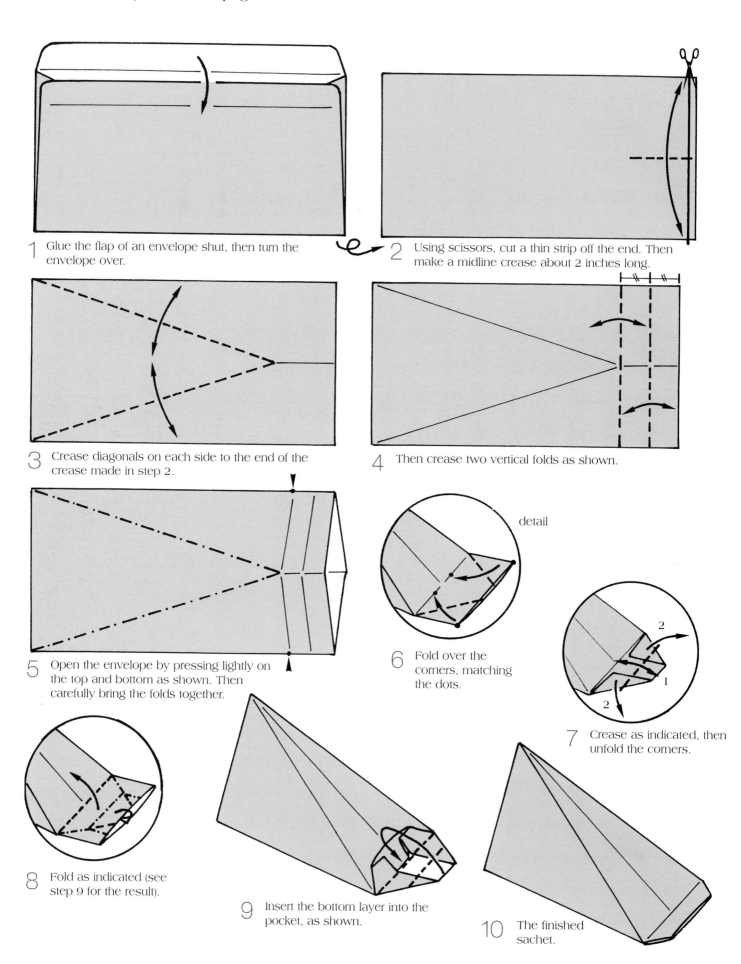

1 Glue the flap of an envelope shut, then turn the envelope over.

2 Using scissors, cut a thin strip off the end. Then make a midline crease about 2 inches long.

3 Crease diagonals on each side to the end of the crease made in step 2.

4 Then crease two vertical folds as shown.

5 Open the envelope by pressing lightly on the top and bottom as shown. Then carefully bring the folds together.

detail

6 Fold over the corners, matching the dots.

7 Crease as indicated, then unfold the corners.

8 Fold as indicated (see step 9 for the result).

9 Insert the bottom layer into the pocket, as shown.

10 The finished sachet.

Sachet

GIFT WRAPPING. You'd never believe how versatile a simple envelope can be. With the flick of the wrist, it becomes a last-minute wrapping for a small gift.

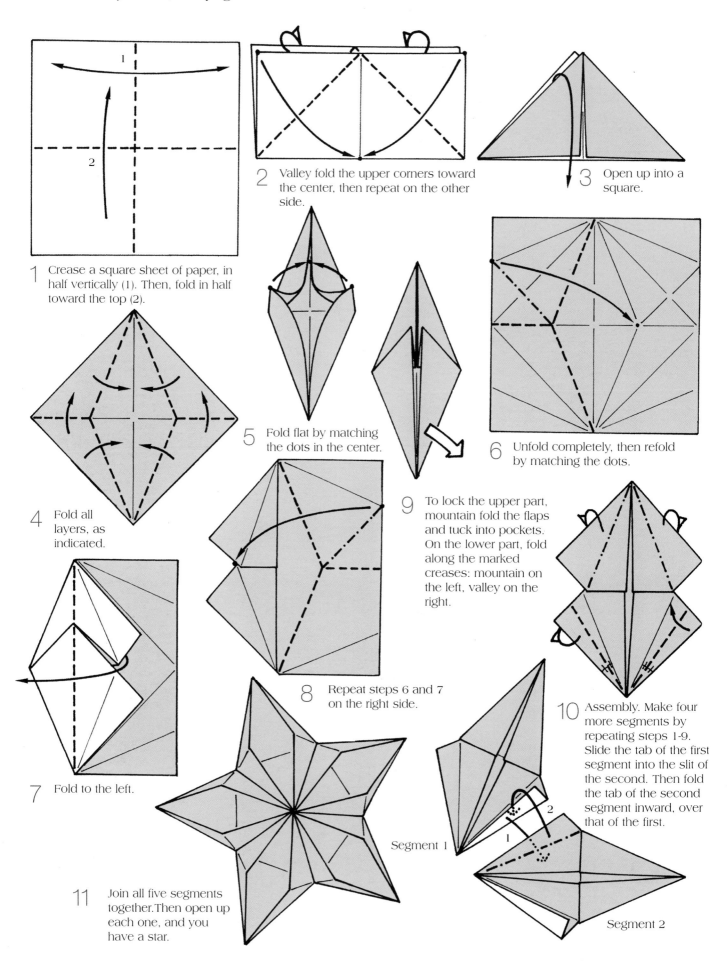

For folds and symbols, see pages 5-9.

1 Crease a square sheet of paper, in half vertically (1). Then, fold in half toward the top (2).

2 Valley fold the upper corners toward the center, then repeat on the other side.

3 Open up into a square.

4 Fold all layers, as indicated.

5 Fold flat by matching the dots in the center.

6 Unfold completely, then refold by matching the dots.

7 Fold to the left.

8 Repeat steps 6 and 7 on the right side.

9 To lock the upper part, mountain fold the flaps and tuck into pockets. On the lower part, fold along the marked creases: mountain on the left, valley on the right.

10 Assembly. Make four more segments by repeating steps 1-9. Slide the tab of the first segment into the slit of the second. Then fold the tab of the second segment inward, over that of the first.

Segment 1

Segment 2

11 Join all five segments together. Then open up each one, and you have a star.

Star-shaped Box

ON THE BRIDGE. The compartments of this nifty star-shaped box hold an assortment of tasty tidbits. This conversation piece is guaranteed to turn your cocktail party into a memorable event.

For folds and symbols, see pages 5-9.

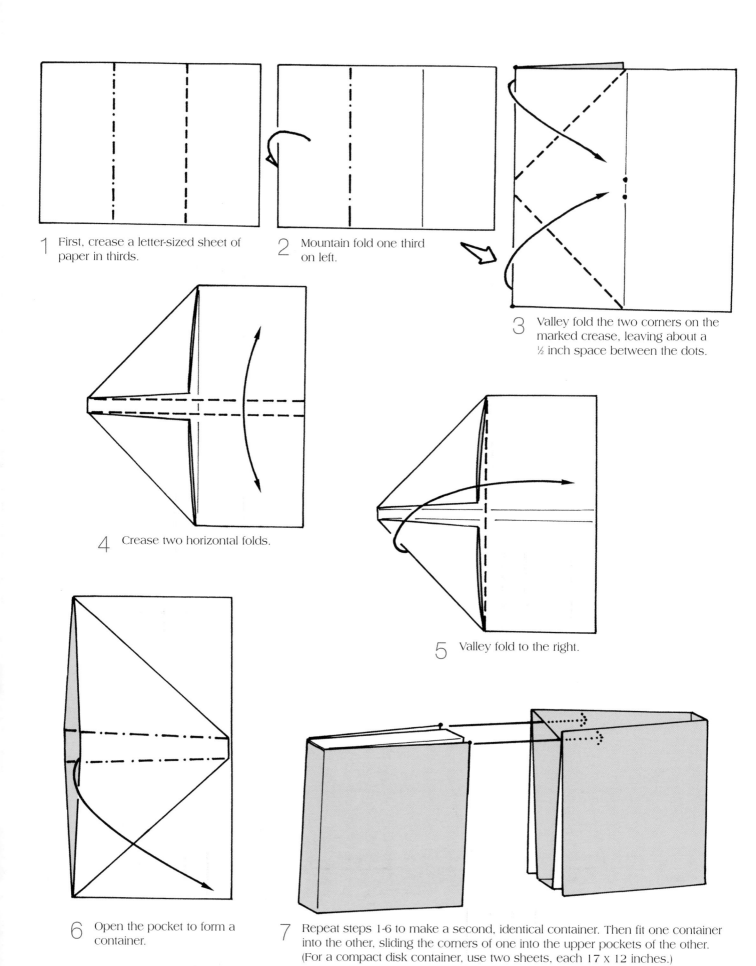

1   First, crease a letter-sized sheet of paper in thirds.

2   Mountain fold one third on left.

3   Valley fold the two corners on the marked crease, leaving about a ½ inch space between the dots.

4   Crease two horizontal folds.

5   Valley fold to the right.

6   Open the pocket to form a container.

7   Repeat steps 1-6 to make a second, identical container. Then fit one container into the other, sliding the corners of one into the upper pockets of the other. (For a compact disk container, use two sheets, each 17 x 12 inches.)

A Box

IN CONCERT. Paper folding is like piano playing...you work with the tips of your fingers and create something magical. It doesn't take a virtuoso to make this useful container. With a little dexterity, even beginners can tackle it—and never hit a false note.

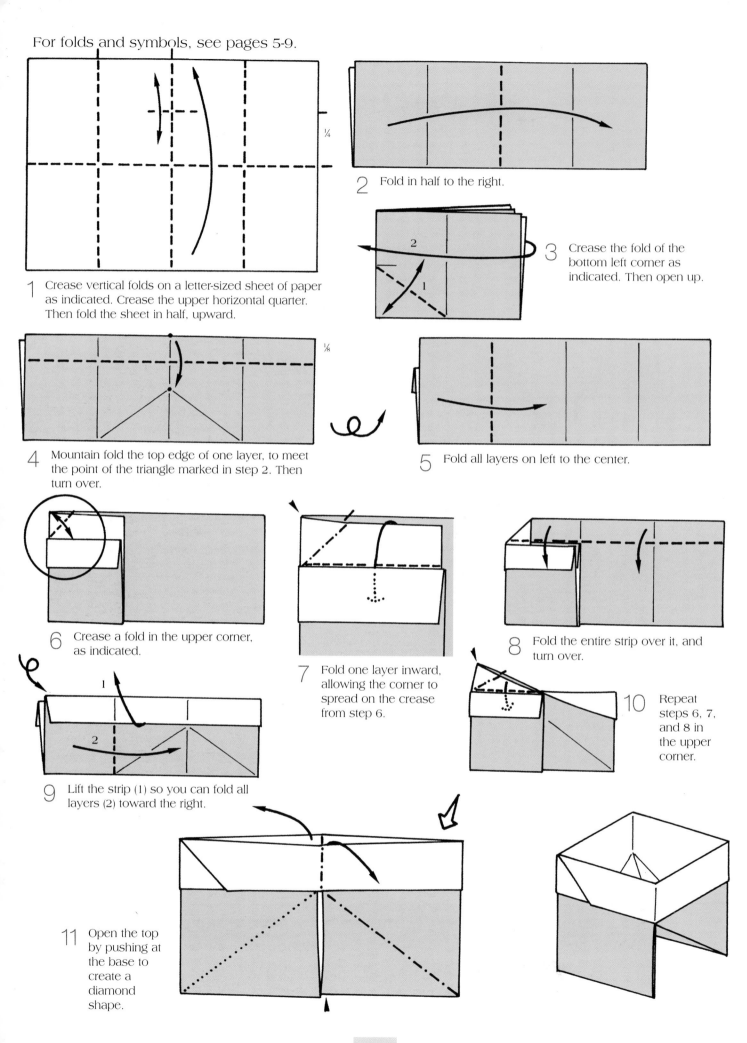

For folds and symbols, see pages 5-9.

¼

1 Crease vertical folds on a letter-sized sheet of paper as indicated. Crease the upper horizontal quarter. Then fold the sheet in half, upward.

2 Fold in half to the right.

3 Crease the fold of the bottom left corner as indicated. Then open up.

⅛

4 Mountain fold the top edge of one layer, to meet the point of the triangle marked in step 2. Then turn over.

5 Fold all layers on left to the center.

6 Crease a fold in the upper corner, as indicated.

7 Fold one layer inward, allowing the corner to spread on the crease from step 6.

8 Fold the entire strip over it, and turn over.

9 Lift the strip (1) so you can fold all layers (2) toward the right.

10 Repeat steps 6, 7, and 8 in the upper corner.

11 Open the top by pushing at the base to create a diamond shape.

Box on Feet

TRUE TO NATURE. Let your imagination take over when you fill a couple of these charming boxes. Use flower petals for potpourri, or multicolored grains to add a rustic touch.

For folds and symbols, see pages 5-9.

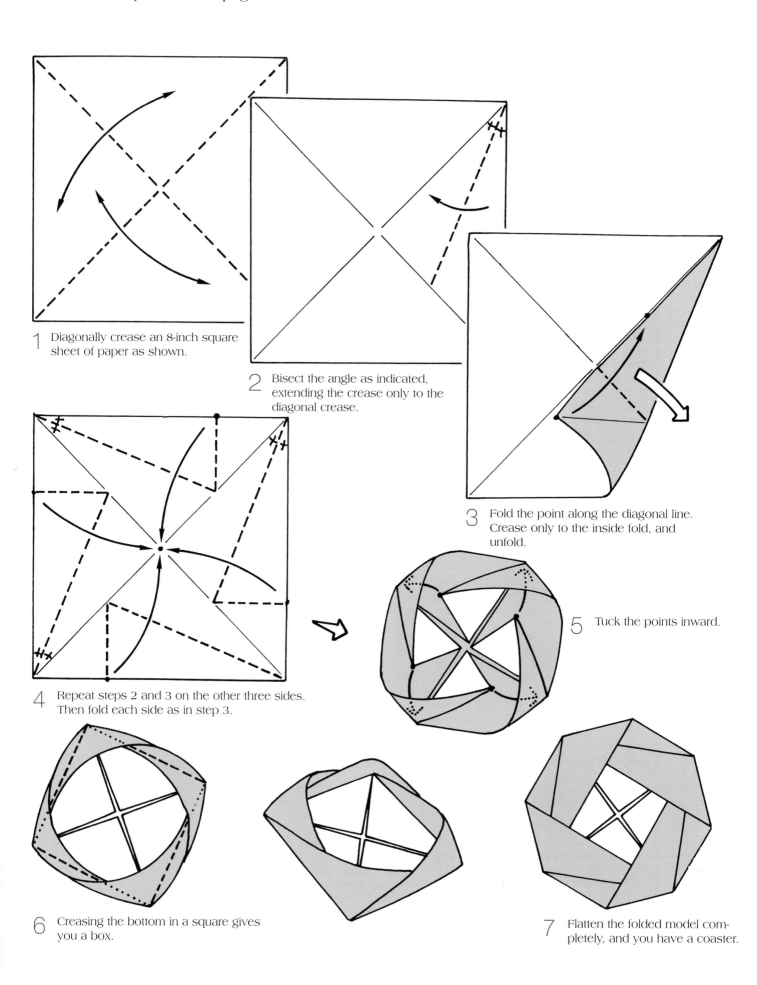

1 Diagonally crease an 8-inch square sheet of paper as shown.

2 Bisect the angle as indicated, extending the crease only to the diagonal crease.

3 Fold the point along the diagonal line. Crease only to the inside fold, and unfold.

4 Repeat steps 2 and 3 on the other three sides. Then fold each side as in step 3.

5 Tuck the points inward.

6 Creasing the bottom in a square gives you a box.

7 Flatten the folded model completely, and you have a coaster.

Mini-container or Coaster

A LITTLE ZEST. Everything is ready. Lemon slices for the drinks, peanuts for nibbling. Now it's time to raise your glass and make a toast to a lovely evening.

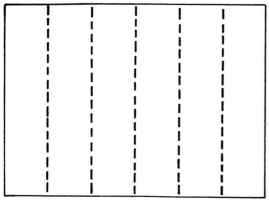

1 Divide a letter-sized sheet of paper into three, then six, equal parts.

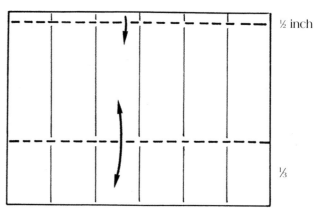

½ inch

⅓

2 Make a ½ inch mountain fold. Fold as shown. Crease the bottom third.

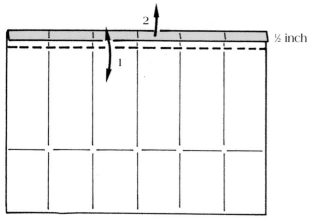

½ inch

3 Make another crease, this one at about ½ inch below the edge of the previous fold, and unfold completely.

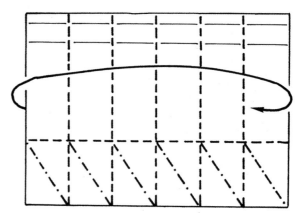

4 At the bottom, mountain crease diagonals through each rectangle. Then roll up, overlapping the two end sections. Form the pentagon of the base by following the folds. (This is a difficult fold. Be patient.)

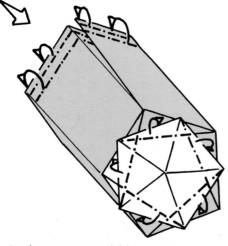

5 On the upper part, fold in on the topmost crease, then again on the next crease; fold each side of the pentagon to shape the whole pencil box.

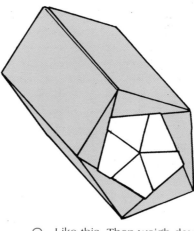

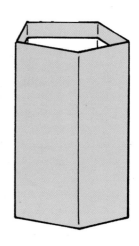

6 Like this. Then weigh down the bottom of the pencil box with sand or small beads.

Pencil Box

BY DESIGN. This model is dedicated to the Japanese artist Shuzo Fujimoto, who is known for his geometrical folds. Weighted down with something solid in the bottom for stability, the pencil box is a good gift for any child who likes to draw.

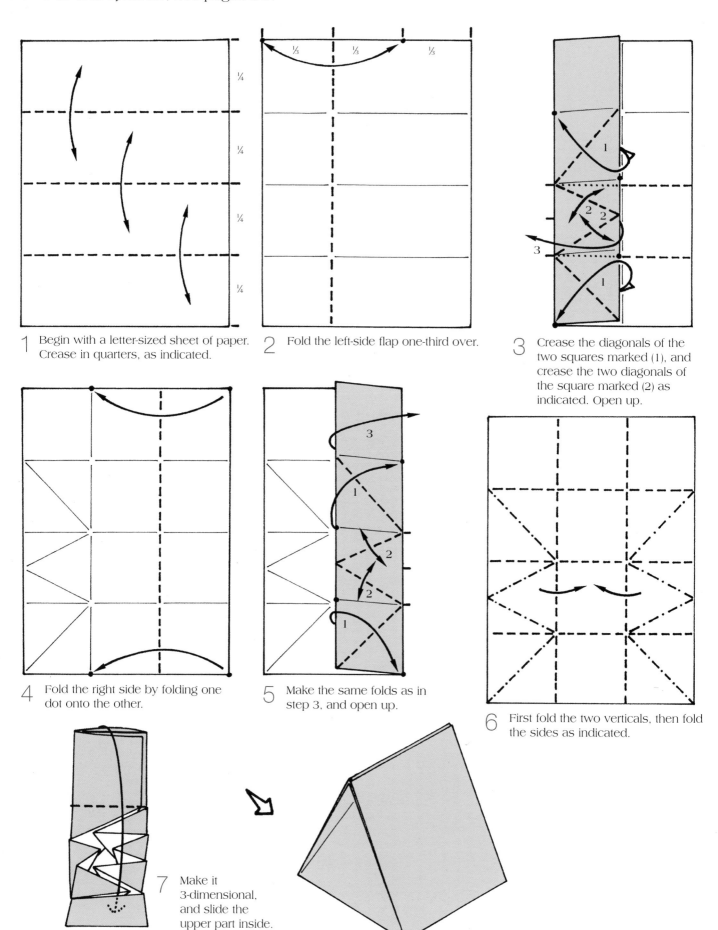

1 Begin with a letter-sized sheet of paper. Crease in quarters, as indicated.

¼
¼
¼
¼

2 Fold the left-side flap one-third over.

⅓ ⅓ ⅓

3 Crease the diagonals of the two squares marked (1), and crease the two diagonals of the square marked (2) as indicated. Open up.

4 Fold the right side by folding one dot onto the other.

5 Make the same folds as in step 3, and open up.

6 First fold the two verticals, then fold the sides as indicated.

7 Make it 3-dimensional, and slide the upper part inside.

Wrapping

IN THE FIELD. Created in a rainbow of colors, these little boxes are just waiting to be filled with the treasures of your choosing.

For folds and symbols, see pages 5-9.

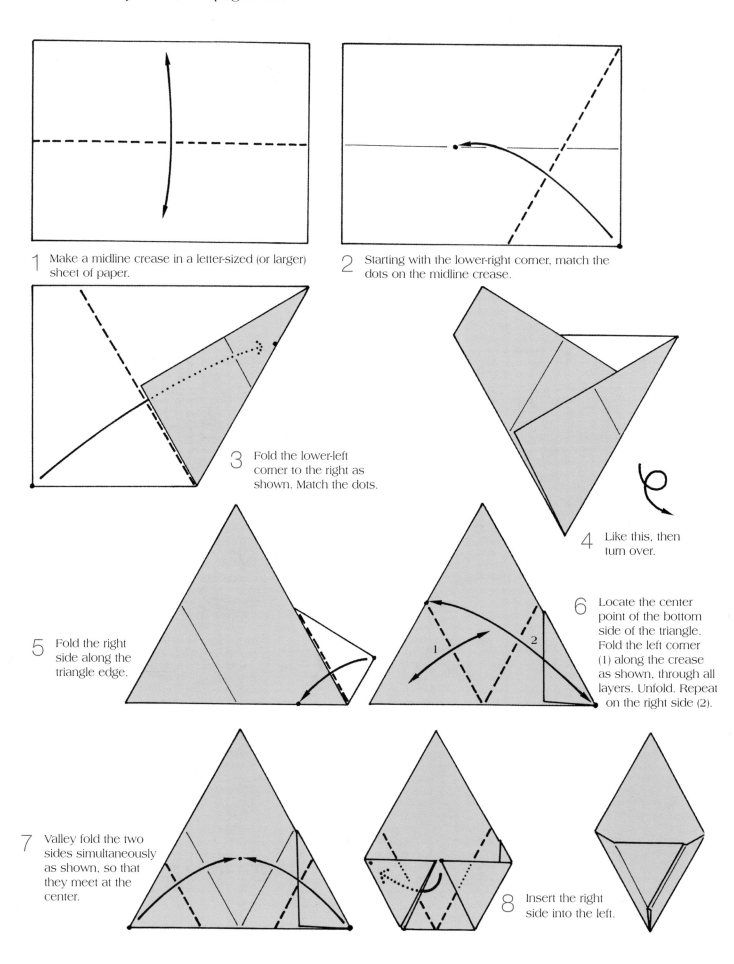

1 Make a midline crease in a letter-sized (or larger) sheet of paper.

2 Starting with the lower-right corner, match the dots on the midline crease.

3 Fold the lower-left corner to the right as shown. Match the dots.

4 Like this, then turn over.

5 Fold the right side along the triangle edge.

6 Locate the center point of the bottom side of the triangle. Fold the left corner (1) along the crease as shown, through all layers. Unfold. Repeat on the right side (2).

7 Valley fold the two sides simultaneously as shown, so that they meet at the center.

8 Insert the right side into the left.

28

Wall Basket

SPICE OF LIFE. This wall fixture fits in Anywhere. Use it to hold fresh herbs and spices that brighten your kitchen and add zip to your meals.

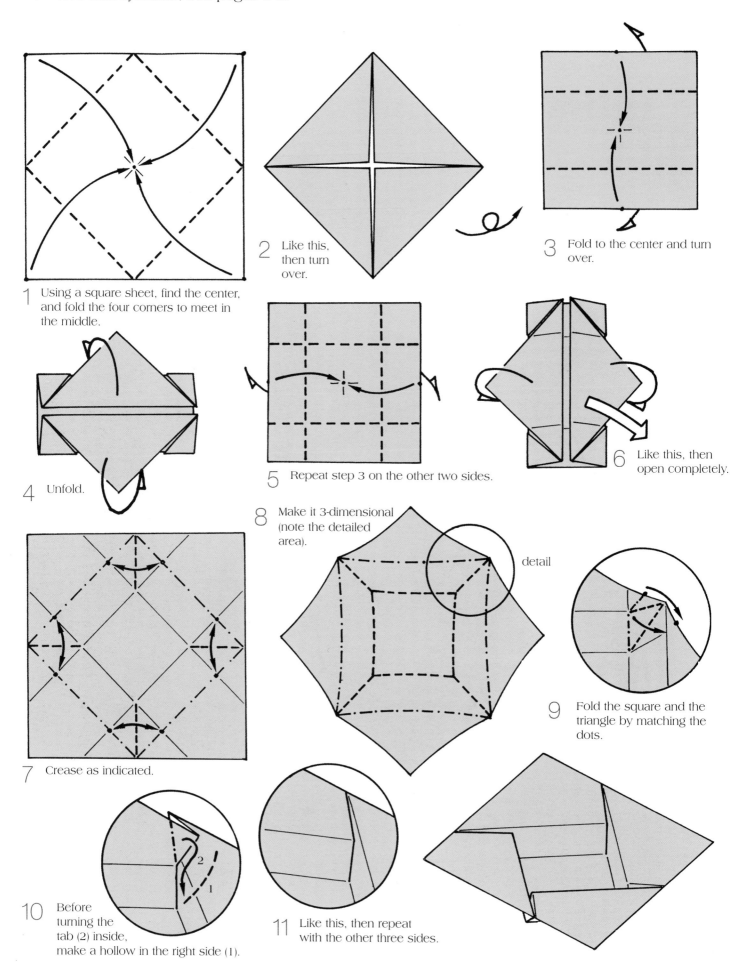

1 Using a square sheet, find the center, and fold the four corners to meet in the middle.

2 Like this, then turn over.

3 Fold to the center and turn over.

4 Unfold.

5 Repeat step 3 on the other two sides.

6 Like this, then open completely.

7 Crease as indicated.

8 Make it 3-dimensional (note the detailed area).

detail

9 Fold the square and the triangle by matching the dots.

10 Before turning the tab (2) inside, make a hollow in the right side (1).

11 Like this, then repeat with the other three sides.

Serving Dish

THE PERFUME OF STAR ANISE. When filling this container, look for something special to complement its simple lines and the color of paper you've selected. Grains or spices should work well.

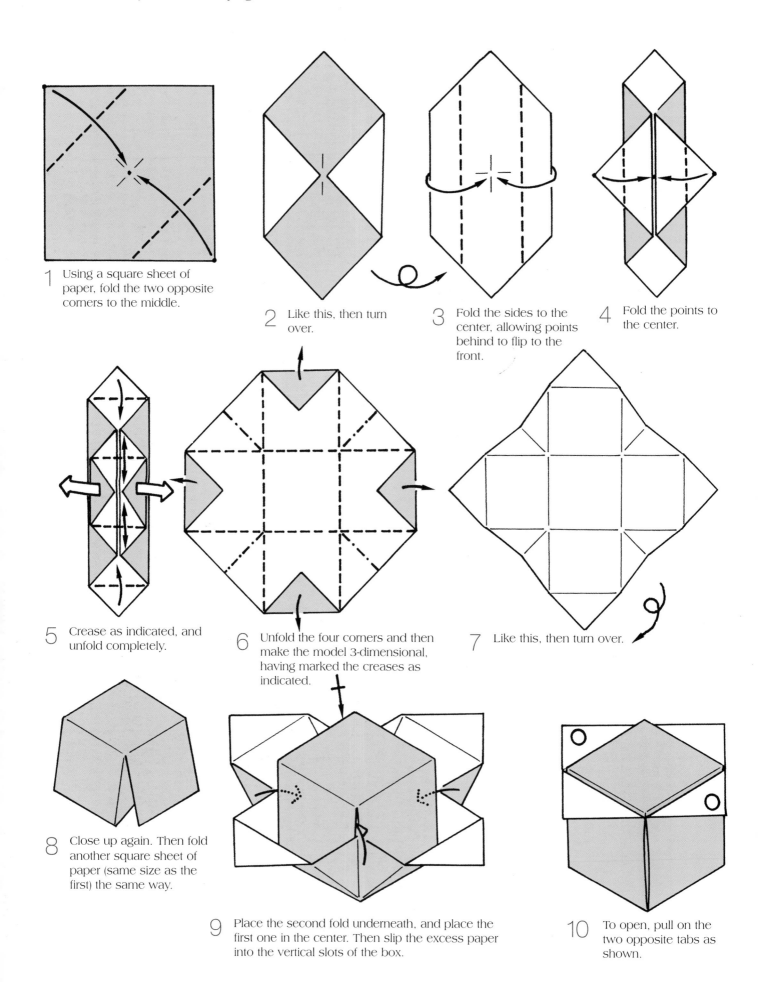

1 Using a square sheet of paper, fold the two opposite corners to the middle.

2 Like this, then turn over.

3 Fold the sides to the center, allowing points behind to flip to the front.

4 Fold the points to the center.

5 Crease as indicated, and unfold completely.

6 Unfold the four corners and then make the model 3-dimensional, having marked the creases as indicated.

7 Like this, then turn over.

8 Close up again. Then fold another square sheet of paper (same size as the first) the same way.

9 Place the second fold underneath, and place the first one in the center. Then slip the excess paper into the vertical slots of the box.

10 To open, pull on the two opposite tabs as shown.

Cube Box

PETALS. The magic of this box lies in the way it opens and closes. Pull the two opposite petals and the cube opens, revealing whatever you've hidden inside.

For folds and symbols, see pages 5-9.

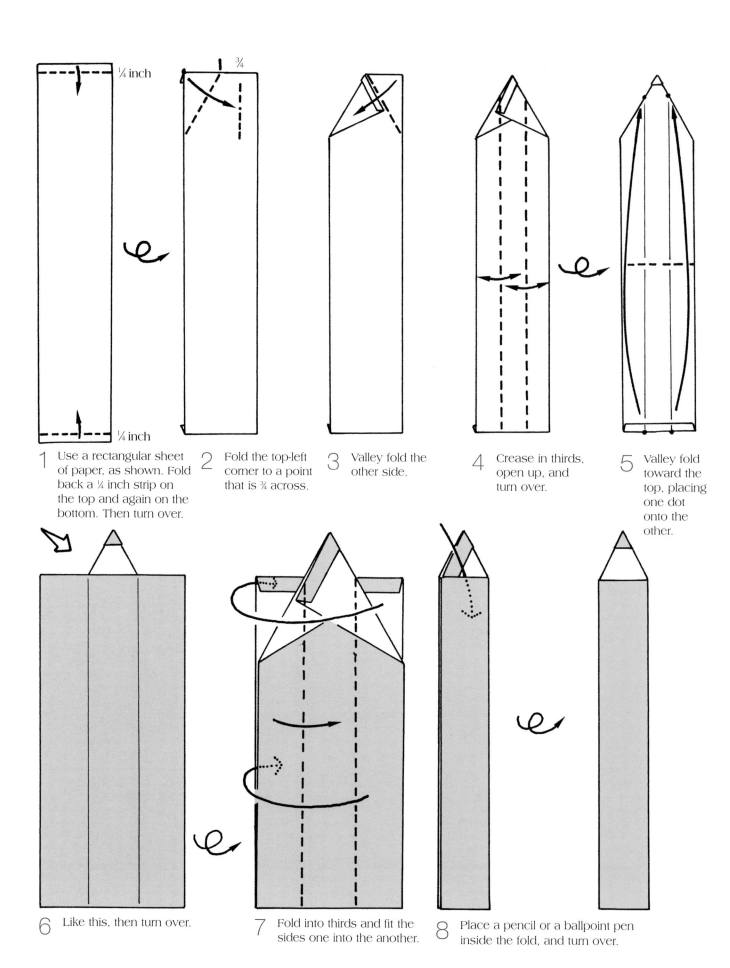

¾

¼ inch

¼ inch

1 Use a rectangular sheet of paper, as shown. Fold back a ¼ inch strip on the top and again on the bottom. Then turn over.

2 Fold the top-left corner to a point that is ¾ across.

3 Valley fold the other side.

4 Crease in thirds, open up, and turn over.

5 Valley fold toward the top, placing one dot onto the other.

6 Like this, then turn over.

7 Fold into thirds and fit the sides one into the another.

8 Place a pencil or a ballpoint pen inside the fold, and turn over.

Pencil Holder

PAPER-WRAPPED PENCILS. What could be more cheerful than a pencil or pen covered in bright paper? A simple ballpoint can be turned into a charming gift for a child or a grown-up. This fold also makes a handy bookmark.

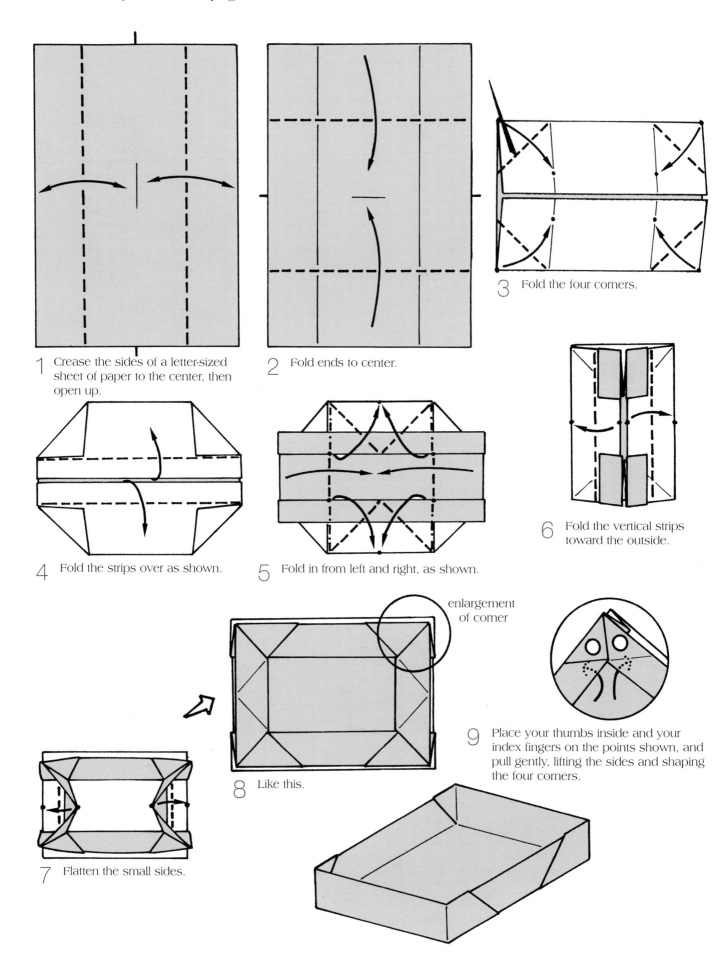

1 Crease the sides of a letter-sized sheet of paper to the center, then open up.

2 Fold ends to center.

3 Fold the four corners.

4 Fold the strips over as shown.

5 Fold in from left and right, as shown.

6 Fold the vertical strips toward the outside.

7 Flatten the small sides.

8 Like this.

enlargement of corner

9 Place your thumbs inside and your index fingers on the points shown, and pull gently, lifting the sides and shaping the four corners.

Rectangular Box

SWEET TOOTH. Who doesn't like sweets...especially when they fill such a delightful box? You can create a cover to protect unwrapped chocolates by following the same steps, but using a slightly smaller piece of paper.

Cards,
Envelopes,
Wallets

For folds and symbols, see pages 5-9.

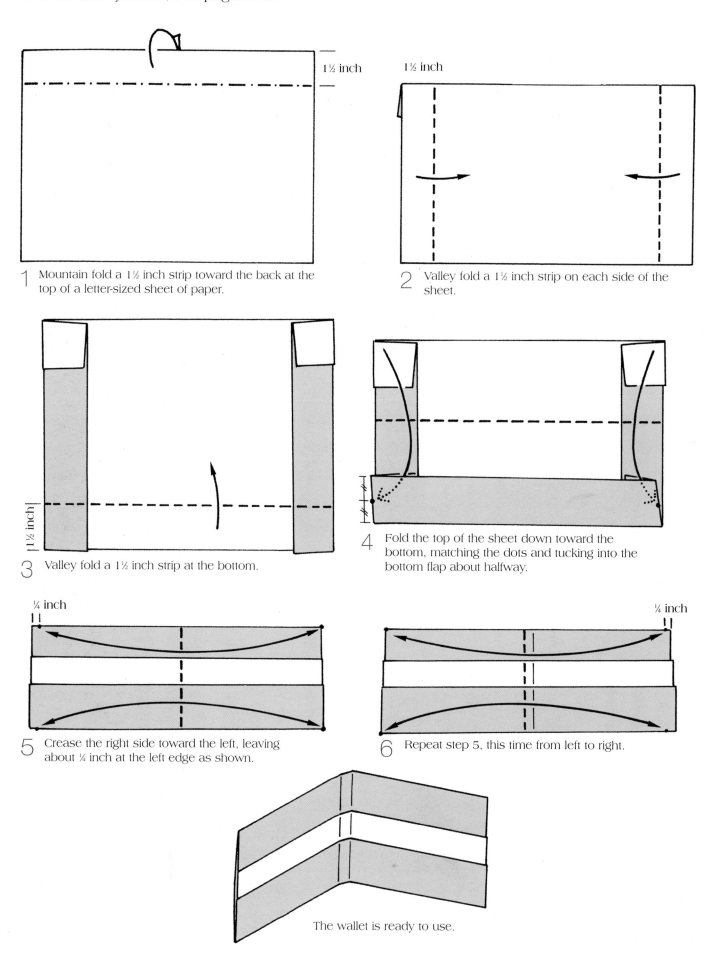

1½ inch

1½ inch   1½ inch

1   Mountain fold a 1½ inch strip toward the back at the top of a letter-sized sheet of paper.

2   Valley fold a 1½ inch strip on each side of the sheet.

1½ inch

3   Valley fold a 1½ inch strip at the bottom.

4   Fold the top of the sheet down toward the bottom, matching the dots and tucking into the bottom flap about halfway.

¼ inch   ¼ inch

5   Crease the right side toward the left, leaving about ¼ inch at the left edge as shown.

¼ inch   ¼ inch

6   Repeat step 5, this time from left to right.

The wallet is ready to use.

40

Wallet

PAPER AND THINGS. All sorts of odds and ends turn up in our pockets at the end of the day. This improvised wallet could hold a dry cleaner's ticket, a bank machine receipt, a shopping list, and a credit card.

For folds and symbols, see pages 5-9.

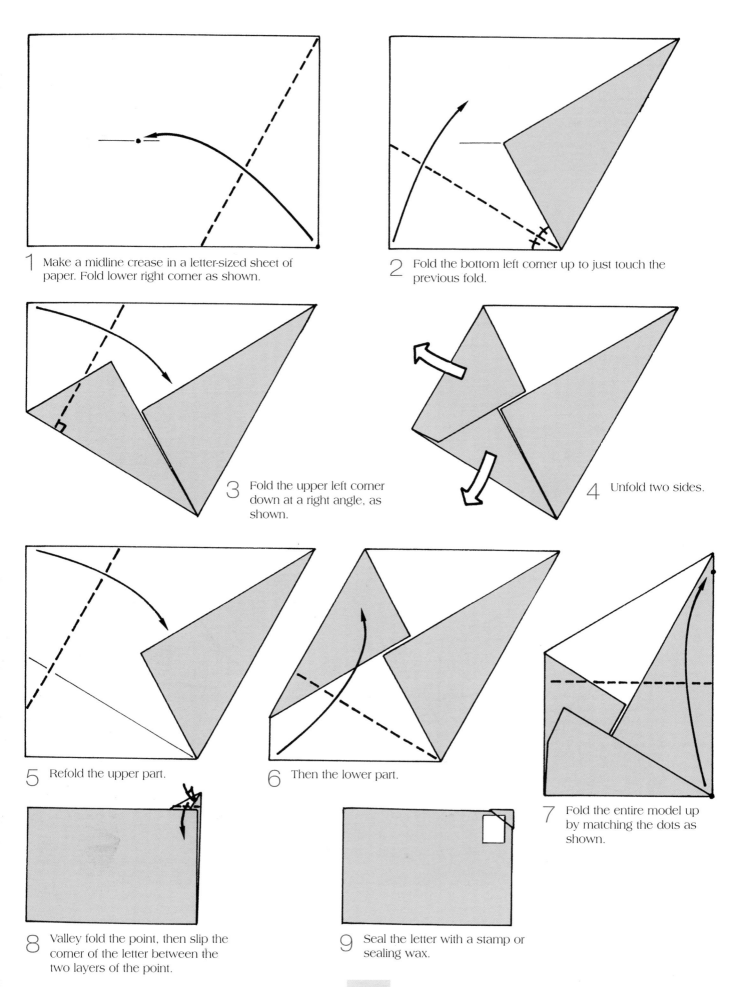

1 Make a midline crease in a letter-sized sheet of paper. Fold lower right corner as shown.

2 Fold the bottom left corner up to just touch the previous fold.

3 Fold the upper left corner down at a right angle, as shown.

4 Unfold two sides.

5 Refold the upper part.

6 Then the lower part.

7 Fold the entire model up by matching the dots as shown.

8 Valley fold the point, then slip the corner of the letter between the two layers of the point.

9 Seal the letter with a stamp or sealing wax.

Envelope

RARE PLEASURE. In this electronic age, it's nice to receive or send an old-fashioned letter. With this fold, you can slide in a post card, or write on the sheet itself before folding it.

For folds and symbols, see pages 5-9.

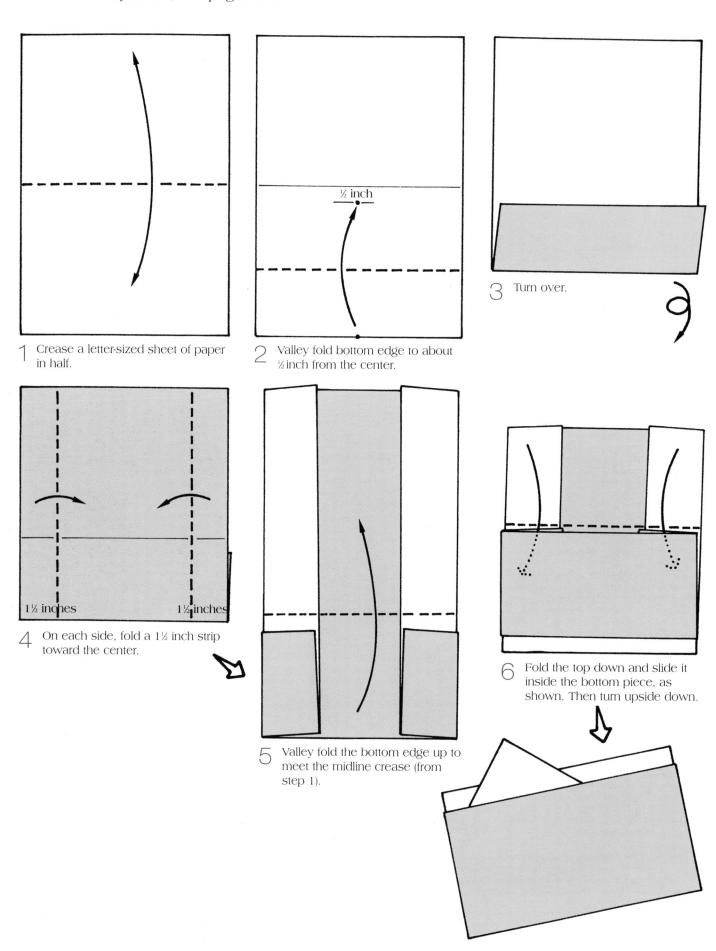

1 Crease a letter-sized sheet of paper in half.

½ inch

2 Valley fold bottom edge to about ½ inch from the center.

3 Turn over.

1½ inches   1½ inches

4 On each side, fold a 1½ inch strip toward the center.

5 Valley fold the bottom edge up to meet the midline crease (from step 1).

6 Fold the top down and slide it inside the bottom piece, as shown. Then turn upside down.

Pouch

MISCELLANEOUS. You'll find this little pouch handy for holding stamps, bus tickets, photographs or anything else that fits.

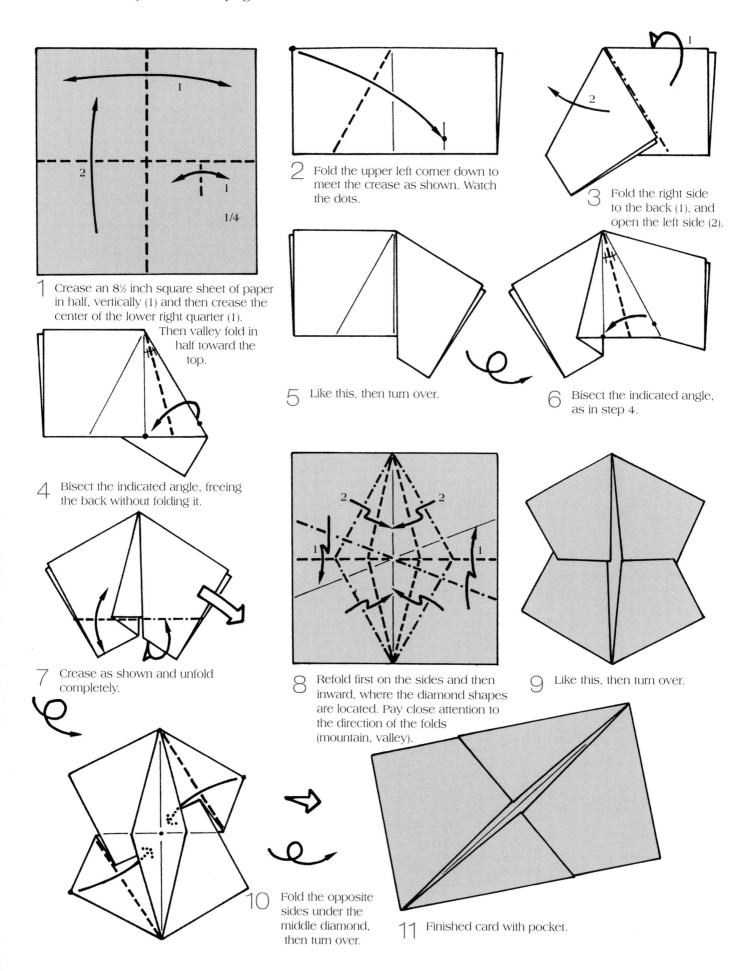

1 Crease an 8½ inch square sheet of paper in half, vertically (1) and then crease the center of the lower right quarter (1). Then valley fold in half toward the top.

1/4

2 Fold the upper left corner down to meet the crease as shown. Watch the dots.

3 Fold the right side to the back (1), and open the left side (2).

4 Bisect the indicated angle, freeing the back without folding it.

5 Like this, then turn over.

6 Bisect the indicated angle, as in step 4.

7 Crease as shown and unfold completely.

8 Refold first on the sides and then inward, where the diamond shapes are located. Pay close attention to the direction of the folds (mountain, valley).

9 Like this, then turn over.

10 Fold the opposite sides under the middle diamond, then turn over.

11 Finished card with pocket.

46

Card with Pocket

SWEET THOUGHTS. Receiving a card with something unexpected inside is a double pleasure. So jot down a few words, then enclose a flower, a picture, or some other little surprise.

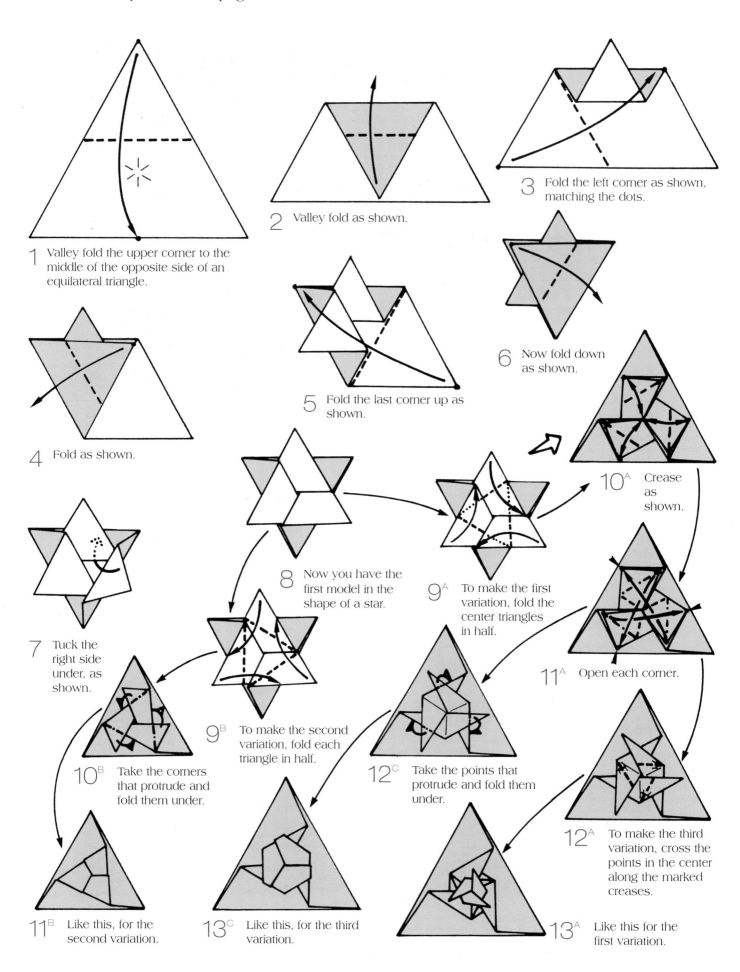

1 Valley fold the upper corner to the middle of the opposite side of an equilateral triangle.

2 Valley fold as shown.

3 Fold the left corner as shown, matching the dots.

4 Fold as shown.

5 Fold the last corner up as shown.

6 Now fold down as shown.

7 Tuck the right side under, as shown.

8 Now you have the first model in the shape of a star.

9^A To make the first variation, fold the center triangles in half.

10^A Crease as shown.

11^A Open each corner.

12^A To make the third variation, cross the points in the center along the marked creases.

13^A Like this for the first variation.

9^B To make the second variation, fold each triangle in half.

10^B Take the corners that protrude and fold them under.

11^B Like this, for the second variation.

12^C Take the points that protrude and fold them under.

13^C Like this, for the third variation.

Messages in a Triangle

LASTING IMPRESSIONS. An astonishing number of geometric configurations are based on the simple triangle. Write a few words before folding, then mail your note to a special friend. Instructions for all three triangles are given here.

For folds and symbols, see pages 5-9.

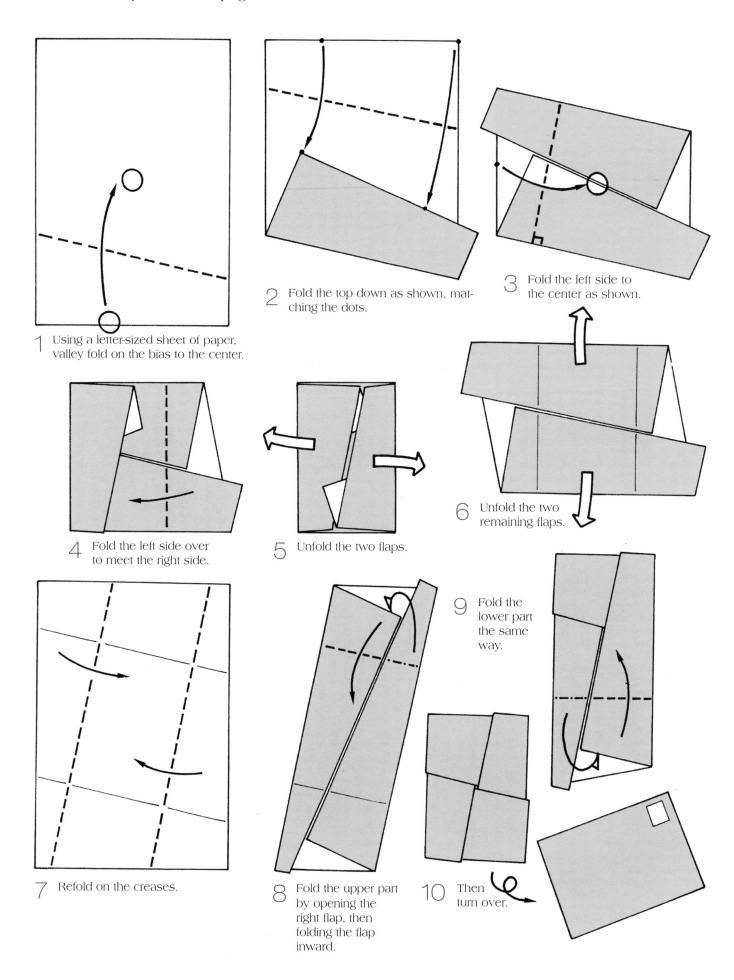

1 Using a letter-sized sheet of paper, valley fold on the bias to the center.

2 Fold the top down as shown, matching the dots.

3 Fold the left side to the center as shown.

4 Fold the left side over to meet the right side.

5 Unfold the two flaps.

6 Unfold the two remaining flaps.

7 Refold on the creases.

8 Fold the upper part by opening the right flap, then folding the flap inward.

9 Fold the lower part the same way.

10 Then turn over.

Letter Envelope

CORRESPONDENCE. Write a short note on a beautiful sheet of paper, then close it up with a few simple folds. A personalized wax seal provides an elegant touch.

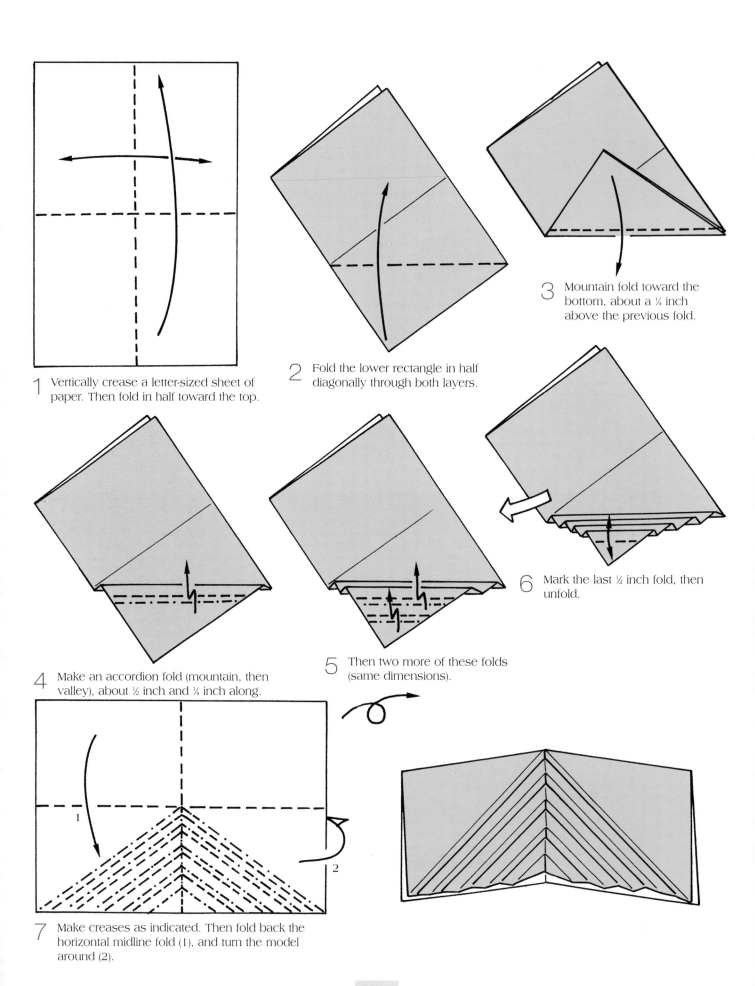

1 Vertically crease a letter-sized sheet of paper. Then fold in half toward the top.

2 Fold the lower rectangle in half diagonally through both layers.

3 Mountain fold toward the bottom, about a ¼ inch above the previous fold.

4 Make an accordion fold (mountain, then valley), about ½ inch and ¼ inch along.

5 Then two more of these folds (same dimensions).

6 Mark the last ½ inch fold, then unfold.

7 Make creases as indicated. Then fold back the horizontal midline fold (1), and turn the model around (2).

Christmas Card

LIGHT SHOW. The folds on this card catch the light and throw off ever-changing shadows. Take pen in hand, then write whatever the moment, or the card, inspires you to say.

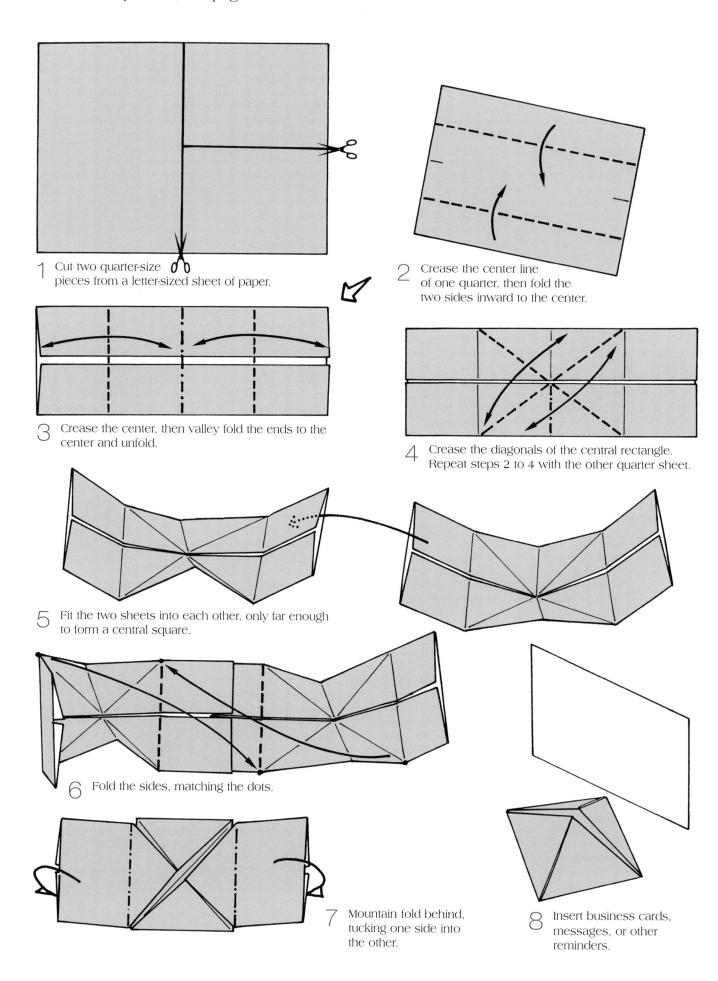

1   Cut two quarter-size pieces from a letter-sized sheet of paper.

2   Crease the center line of one quarter, then fold the two sides inward to the center.

3   Crease the center, then valley fold the ends to the center and unfold.

4   Crease the diagonals of the central rectangle. Repeat steps 2 to 4 with the other quarter sheet.

5   Fit the two sheets into each other, only far enough to form a central square.

6   Fold the sides, matching the dots.

7   Mountain fold behind, tucking one side into the other.

8   Insert business cards, messages, or other reminders.

Card Holder

REMINDERS. You sometimes spend forever searching for business cards and appointment reminders. This little holder can be extremely handy.

For folds and symbols, see pages 5-9.

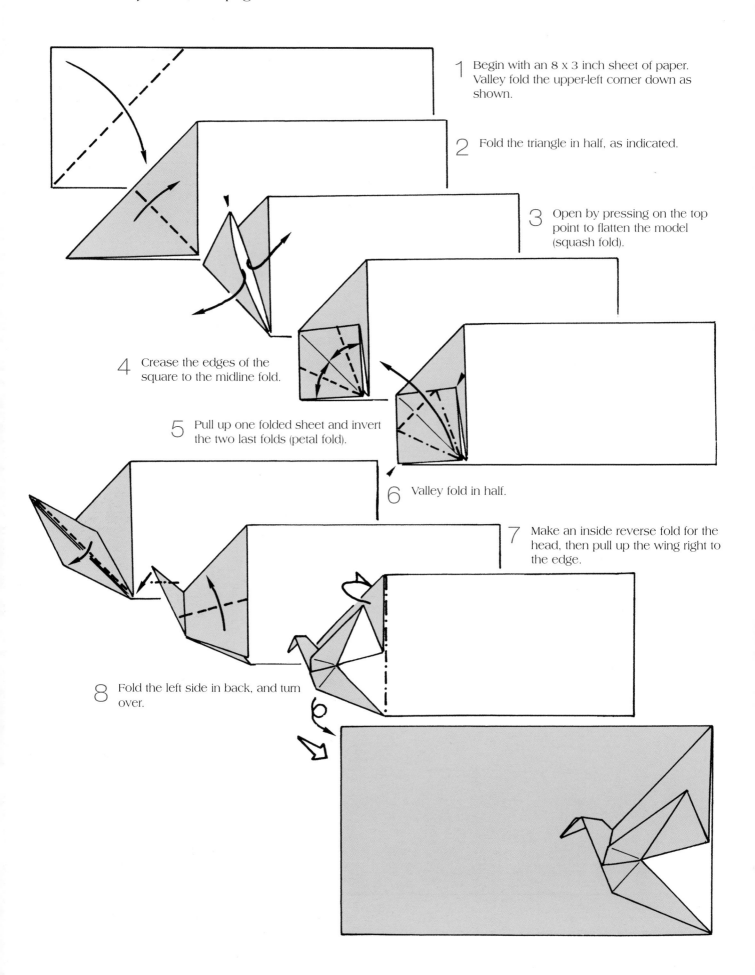

1 Begin with an 8 x 3 inch sheet of paper. Valley fold the upper-left corner down as shown.

2 Fold the triangle in half, as indicated.

3 Open by pressing on the top point to flatten the model (squash fold).

4 Crease the edges of the square to the midline fold.

5 Pull up one folded sheet and invert the two last folds (petal fold).

6 Valley fold in half.

7 Make an inside reverse fold for the head, then pull up the wing right to the edge.

8 Fold the left side in back, and turn over.

56

New Year's Greetings

TRADITION. In Japan on New Year's Day, people play an ancient card game called "Songs of One Hundred Poets." They also send greeting cards, like this one in the shape of a crane...the symbol of peace and good fortune.

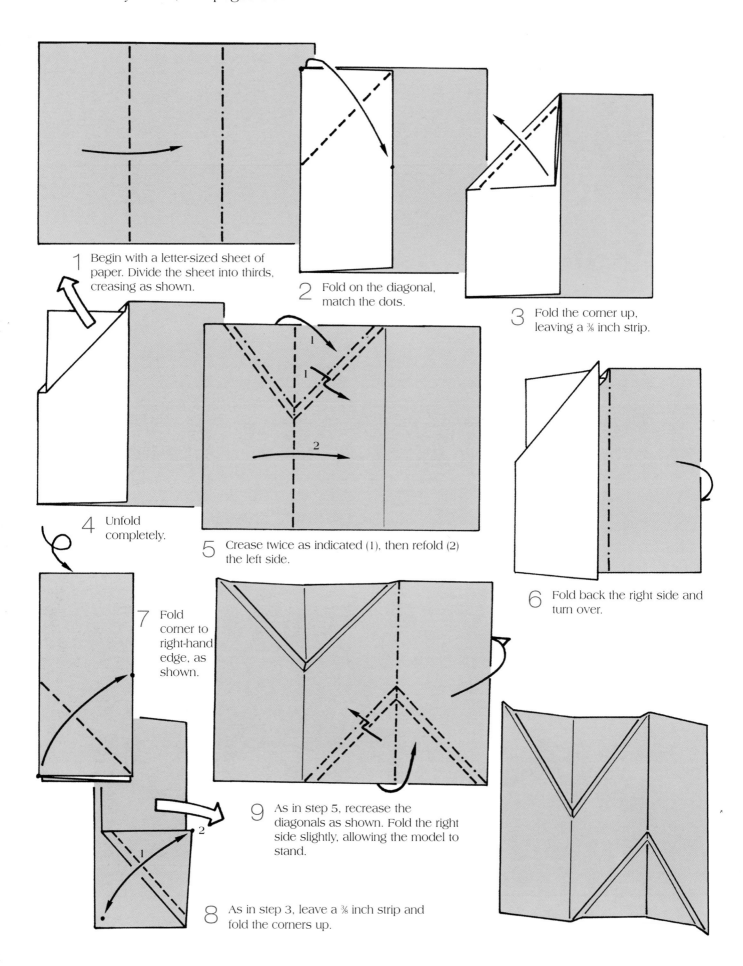

1 Begin with a letter-sized sheet of paper. Divide the sheet into thirds, creasing as shown.

2 Fold on the diagonal, match the dots.

3 Fold the corner up, leaving a ⅜ inch strip.

4 Unfold completely.

5 Crease twice as indicated (1), then refold (2) the left side.

6 Fold back the right side and turn over.

7 Fold corner to right-hand edge, as shown.

8 As in step 3, leave a ⅜ inch strip and fold the corners up.

9 As in step 5, recrease the diagonals as shown. Fold the right side slightly, allowing the model to stand.

Invitations

YIN AND YANG. This card plays with opposing but complementary principles: positive, negative; full, empty; up, down; over, under. Personalize your invitations by writing a special message on each one you send out.

For folds and symbols, see pages 5-9.

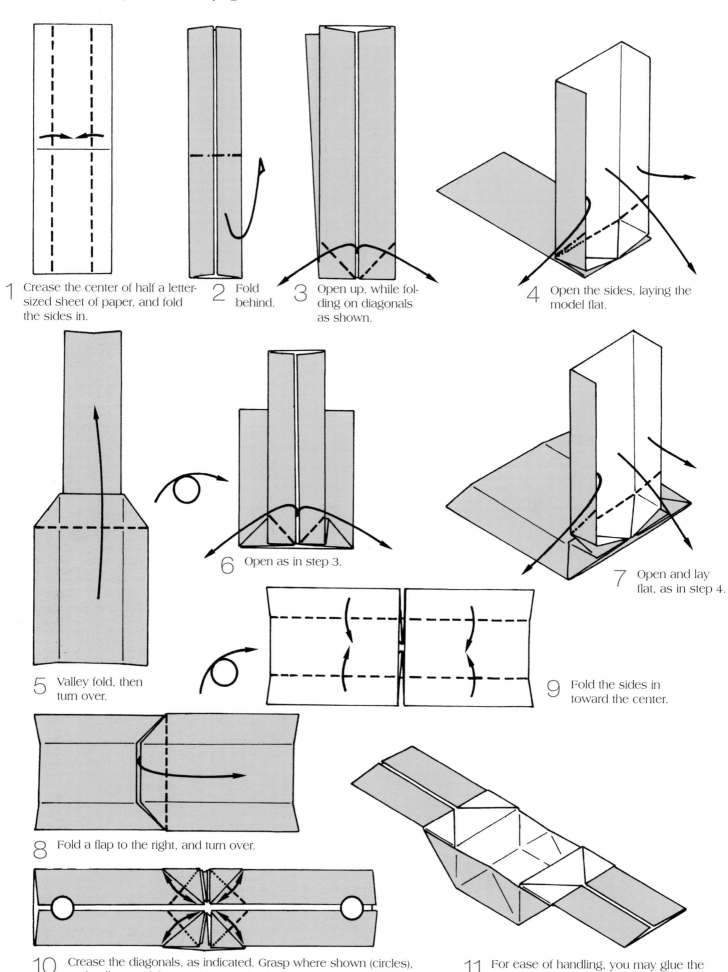

1 Crease the center of half a letter-sized sheet of paper, and fold the sides in.

2 Fold behind.

3 Open up, while folding on diagonals as shown.

4 Open the sides, laying the model flat.

5 Valley fold, then turn over.

6 Open as in step 3.

7 Open and lay flat, as in step 4.

8 Fold a flap to the right, and turn over.

9 Fold the sides in toward the center.

10 Crease the diagonals, as indicated. Grasp where shown (circles), and pull toward the outside to make the box appear.

11 For ease of handling, you may glue the sides up to the marked creases.

60

Box Card

SURPRISE. This card looks flat but it hides a box, which appears when you pull on the ends. Use it to hold a message or a calling card.

For folds and symbols, see pages 5-9.

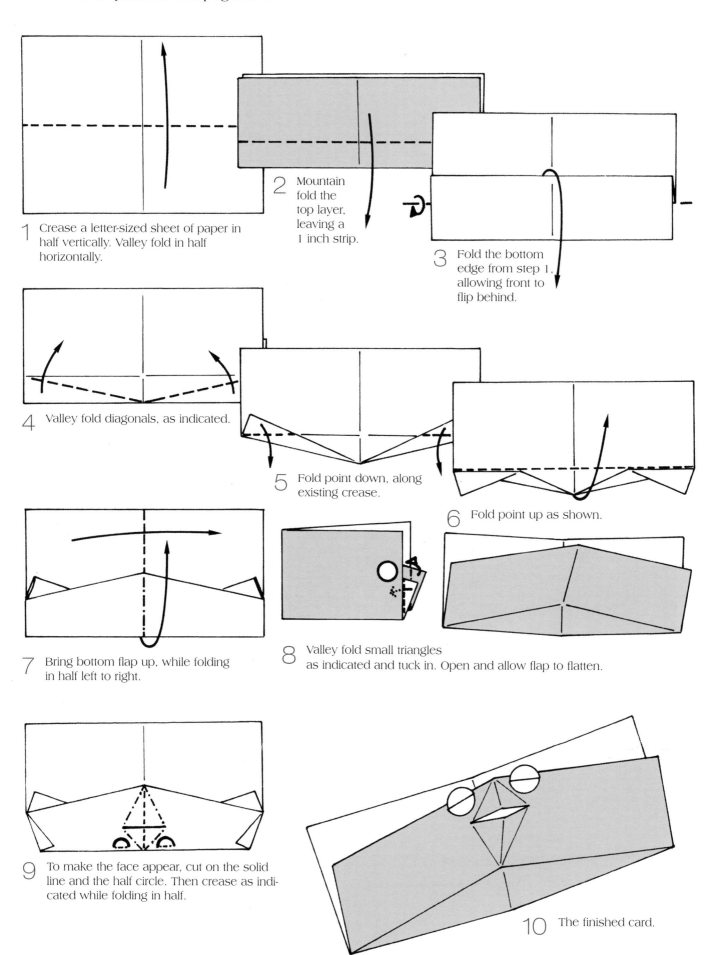

1 Crease a letter-sized sheet of paper in half vertically. Valley fold in half horizontally.

2 Mountain fold the top layer, leaving a 1 inch strip.

3 Fold the bottom edge from step 1, allowing front to flip behind.

4 Valley fold diagonals, as indicated.

5 Fold point down, along existing crease.

6 Fold point up as shown.

7 Bring bottom flap up, while folding in half left to right.

8 Valley fold small triangles as indicated and tuck in. Open and allow flap to flatten.

9 To make the face appear, cut on the solid line and the half circle. Then crease as indicated while folding in half.

10 The finished card.

Pop-up Card

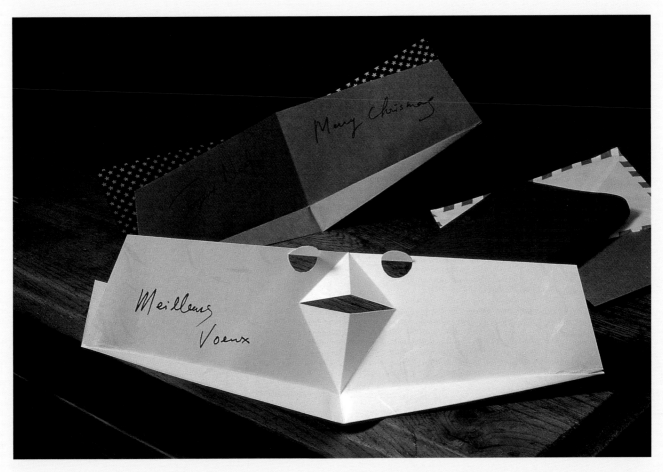

ANIMATED FELLOW. This card was created on the pop-up principle used in children's books. When you open it, a fold pops up. A few simple cuts give life to this little fellow. Watch him move his lips when you open the card.

For folds and symbols, see pages 5-9.

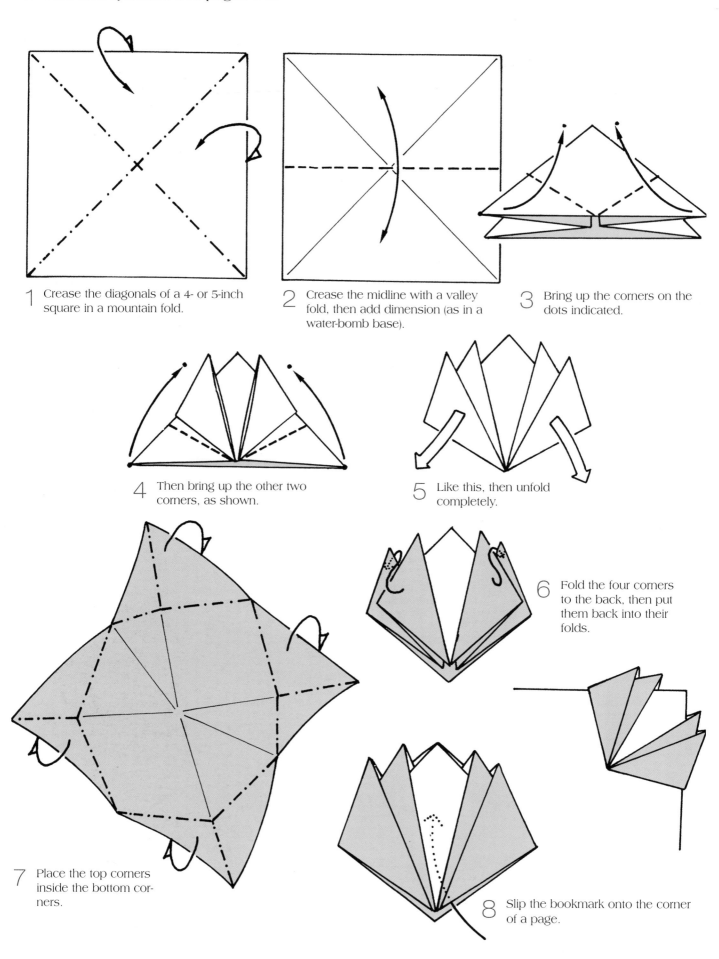

1 Crease the diagonals of a 4- or 5-inch square in a mountain fold.

2 Crease the midline with a valley fold, then add dimension (as in a water-bomb base).

3 Bring up the corners on the dots indicated.

4 Then bring up the other two corners, as shown.

5 Like this, then unfold completely.

6 Fold the four corners to the back, then put them back into their folds.

7 Place the top corners inside the bottom corners.

8 Slip the bookmark onto the corner of a page.

64

Bookmark

HOLD THAT PAGE. The little lotus flower keeps you company when you read. It slips easily on the corner of a page, reminding you where you stopped reading.

Airplanes and Helicopters

For folds and symbols, see pages 5-9.

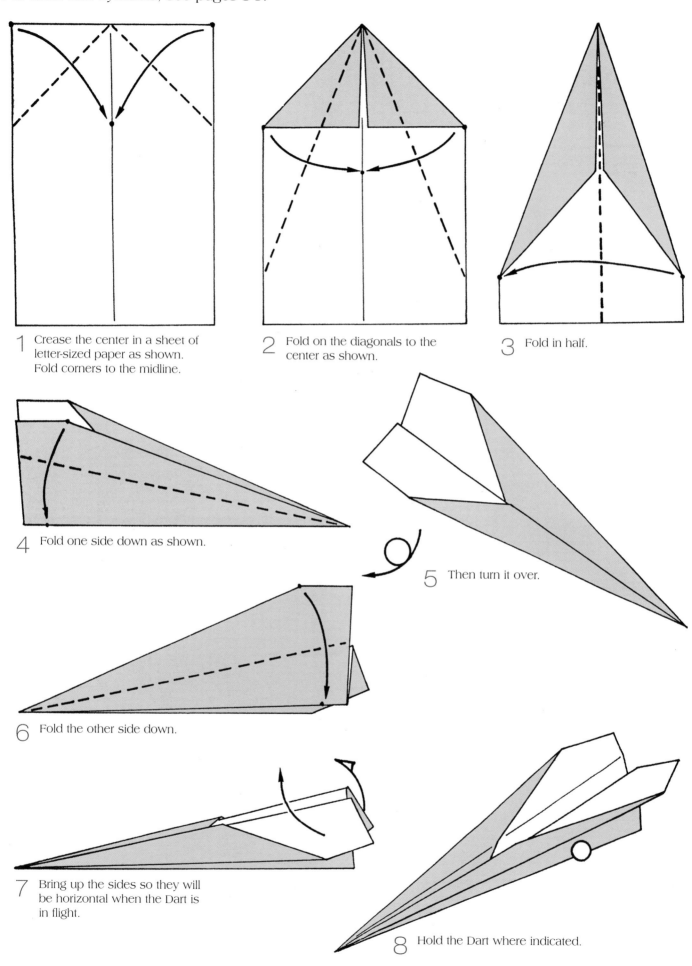

1 Crease the center in a sheet of letter-sized paper as shown. Fold corners to the midline.

2 Fold on the diagonals to the center as shown.

3 Fold in half.

4 Fold one side down as shown.

5 Then turn it over.

6 Fold the other side down.

7 Bring up the sides so they will be horizontal when the Dart is in flight.

8 Hold the Dart where indicated.

Dart

GOOD FLIGHT RECORD. Among the airborne folds, the Dart is probably the best known, thanks to the simplicity of its design and its consistent performance.

1 Fold the bottom right corner of a letter-sized sheet of paper up as shown.

2 Cut off the strip at the top and unfold the square.

3 Crease the top strip in half, and fold the square along the diagonals as indicated.

5 Fold the other two corners of the strip.

4 Fold the edges of the strip to the center crease, while folding corners as indicated. Fold the points of the triangle down to the bottom.

6 Fold the angle bisectors, as indicated (rabbit-ear fold). The model will not lie flat at this point.

8 To launch the plane, fold the model in two.

7 Insert the strip down to the point, and mountain fold the point in two.

Schoolboy

LEARNING TO FLY. The folding technique for this plane is sophisticated, but should not present any difficulties. The thickness of the Schoolboy's nose makes this plane a good outdoor flyer.

For folds and symbols, see pages 5-9.

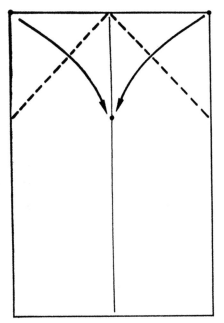

1 Crease the center of a sheet of letter-sized paper lengthwise. Fold corners to the midline.

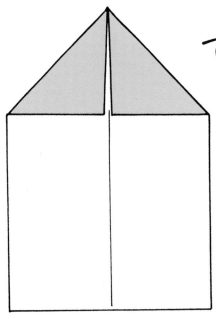

2 Like this, then turn over.

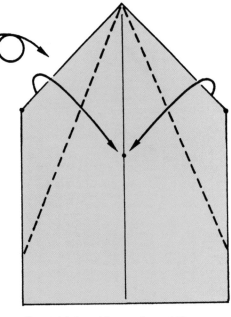

3 Fold the sides to the midline crease along the diagonal, and free the back.

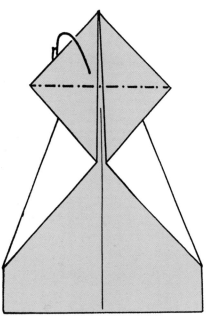

4 Mountain fold the top toward the back as shown.

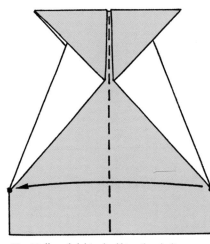

5 Valley fold in half to the left.

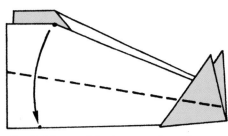

6 Fold one side down to the edge.

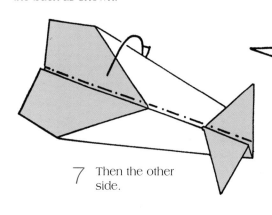

7 Then the other side.

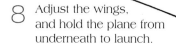

8 Adjust the wings, and hold the plane from underneath to launch.

Duck Plane

SOARING! This plane first took off in 1907, with its rudder in the back. Its contemporary paper version flies extremely well.

For folds and symbols, see pages 5-9.

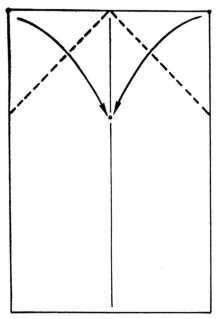

1 Crease the center of a sheet of letter-sized paper lengthwise. Fold corners to the midline.

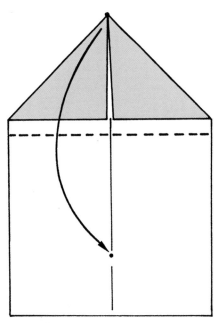

2 Valley fold the top point down onto the center line, leaving a strip as shown.

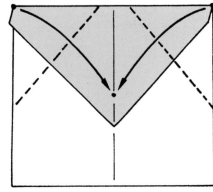

3 Then fold the points to the middle along the diagonals shown. (Folds do not meet, except at points.)

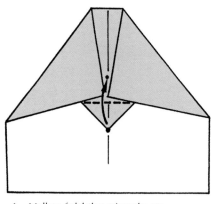

4 Valley fold the triangle up.

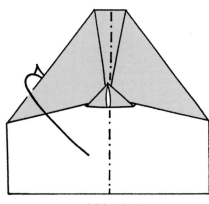

5 Mountain fold in half.

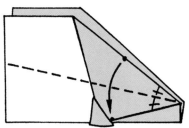

6 Fold one side down, dividing the angle in half.

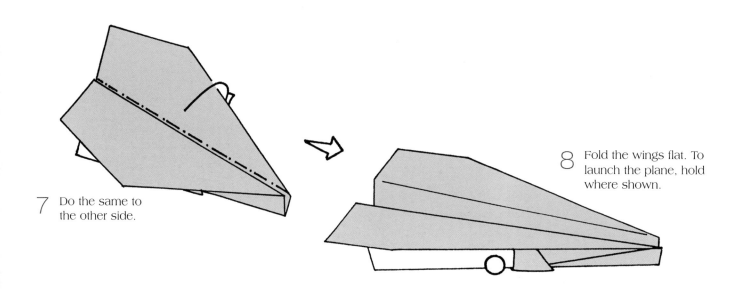

7 Do the same to the other side.

8 Fold the wings flat. To launch the plane, hold where shown.

Glider

HAPPY LANDINGS. Originating in China, this airplane went on to become a favorite in Europe and the rest of the world. Like the real aircraft, the paper model flies gracefully and lands very gently.

For folds and symbols, see pages 5-9.

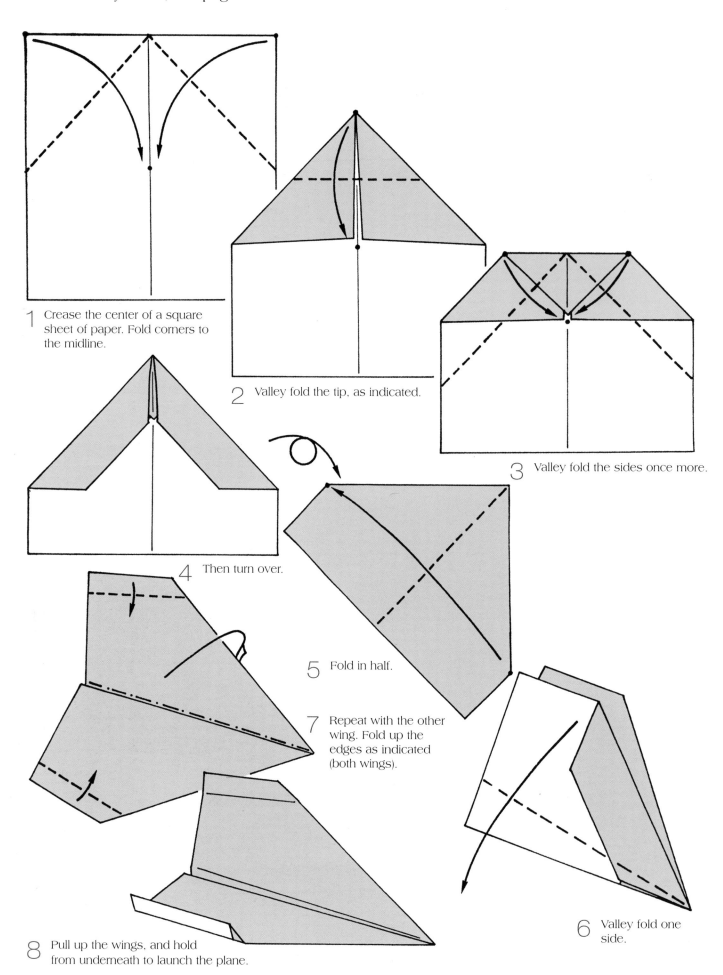

1 Crease the center of a square sheet of paper. Fold corners to the midline.

2 Valley fold the tip, as indicated.

3 Valley fold the sides once more.

4 Then turn over.

5 Fold in half.

6 Valley fold one side.

7 Repeat with the other wing. Fold up the edges as indicated (both wings).

8 Pull up the wings, and hold from underneath to launch the plane.

Overflight

NO TURBULENCE. This traditional model is Japanese. Its wings provide exceptional flight stability. Let your imagination take flight, and sail your plane over uncharted territories.

For folds and symbols, see pages 5-9.

1 Crease the center of a 3 x 5 inch square sheet of paper.

2 Fold in thirds to the center.

3 Mountain fold in half.

4 Crease the corner and then fold a flap to the left, as indicated.

5 Mountain fold behind.

6 Fold up one sheet.

View 7 (profile)

7 Crease the edges, and fold in half in the back.

8 To launch the plane, hold where shown.

Looping

AIR SHOW. This model begins with a small square of paper. Stretch out your arm when you let it fly. Your plane will perform some airborne acrobatics before landing a few yards away.

For folds and symbols, see pages 5-9.

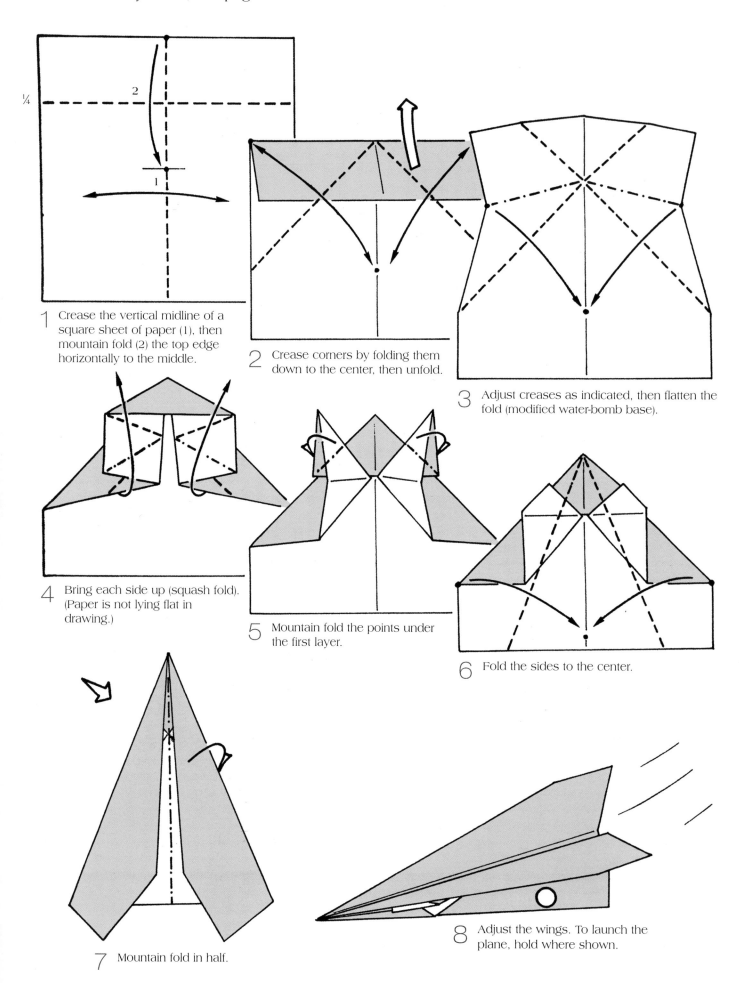

1 Crease the vertical midline of a square sheet of paper (1), then mountain fold (2) the top edge horizontally to the middle.

2 Crease corners by folding them down to the center, then unfold.

3 Adjust creases as indicated, then flatten the fold (modified water-bomb base).

4 Bring each side up (squash fold). (Paper is not lying flat in drawing.)

5 Mountain fold the points under the first layer.

6 Fold the sides to the center.

7 Mountain fold in half.

8 Adjust the wings. To launch the plane, hold where shown.

Ready to Land

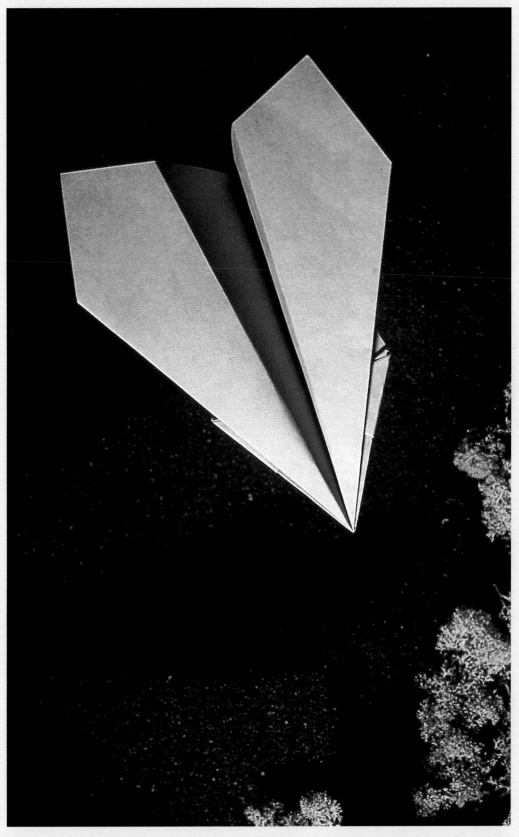

FAR AND AWAY. This plane resembles the Dart, but its nose is reinforced by several layers of paper. So it flies exceptionally smoothly, and surprisingly far.

For folds and symbols, see pages 5-9.

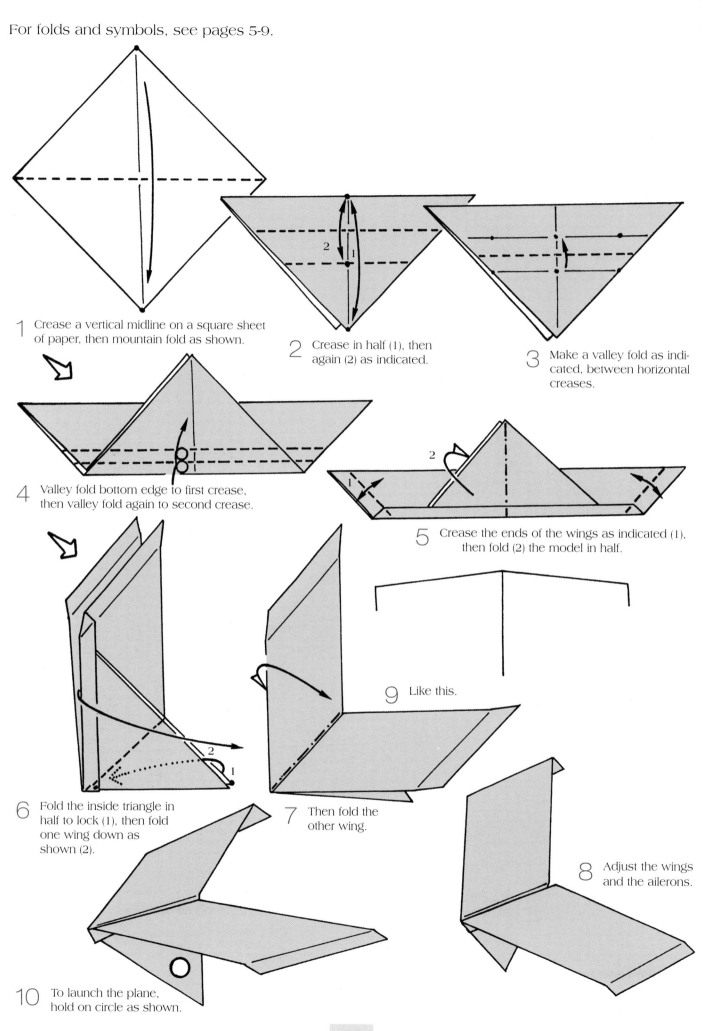

1 Crease a vertical midline on a square sheet of paper, then mountain fold as shown.

2 Crease in half (1), then again (2) as indicated.

3 Make a valley fold as indicated, between horizontal creases.

4 Valley fold bottom edge to first crease, then valley fold again to second crease.

5 Crease the ends of the wings as indicated (1), then fold (2) the model in half.

6 Fold the inside triangle in half to lock (1), then fold one wing down as shown (2).

7 Then fold the other wing.

8 Adjust the wings and the ailerons.

9 Like this.

10 To launch the plane, hold on circle as shown.

Globetrotter

MINOR ADJUSTMENTS. To be sure the plane flies smoothly, carefully adjust its wings and stabilizer each time you launch it. It's the stabilizer that allows such an even performance.

For folds and symbols, see pages 5-9.

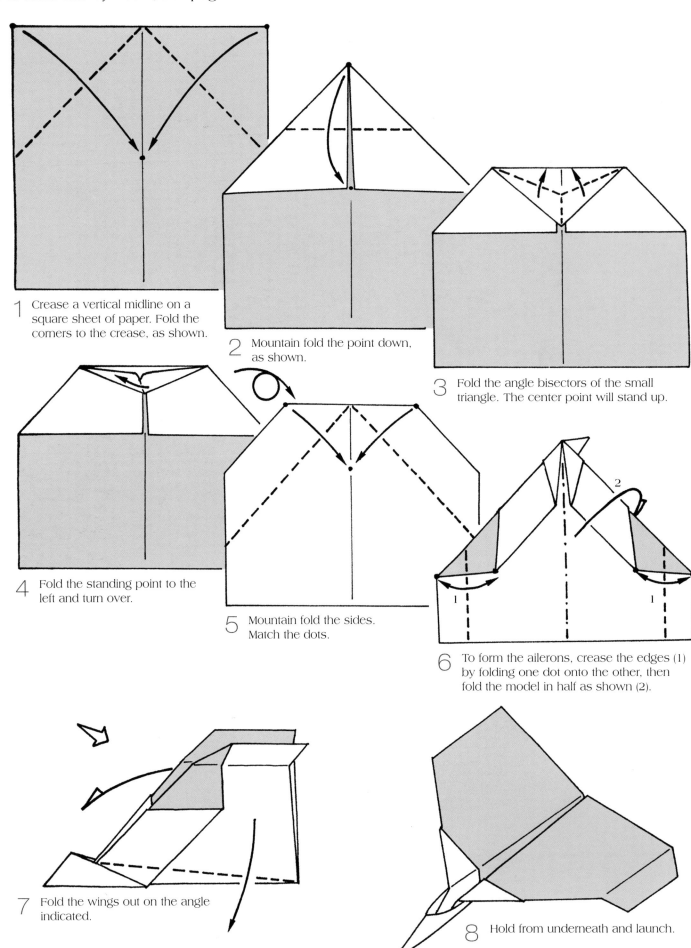

1 Crease a vertical midline on a square sheet of paper. Fold the corners to the crease, as shown.

2 Mountain fold the point down, as shown.

3 Fold the angle bisectors of the small triangle. The center point will stand up.

4 Fold the standing point to the left and turn over.

5 Mountain fold the sides. Match the dots.

6 To form the ailerons, crease the edges (1) by folding one dot onto the other, then fold the model in half as shown (2).

7 Fold the wings out on the angle indicated.

8 Hold from underneath and launch.

Ready for Takeoff

DEPARTURE TIME. This model is remarkably simple to fold. Wide wings help it fly slowly and gracefully.

For folds and symbols, see pages 5-9.

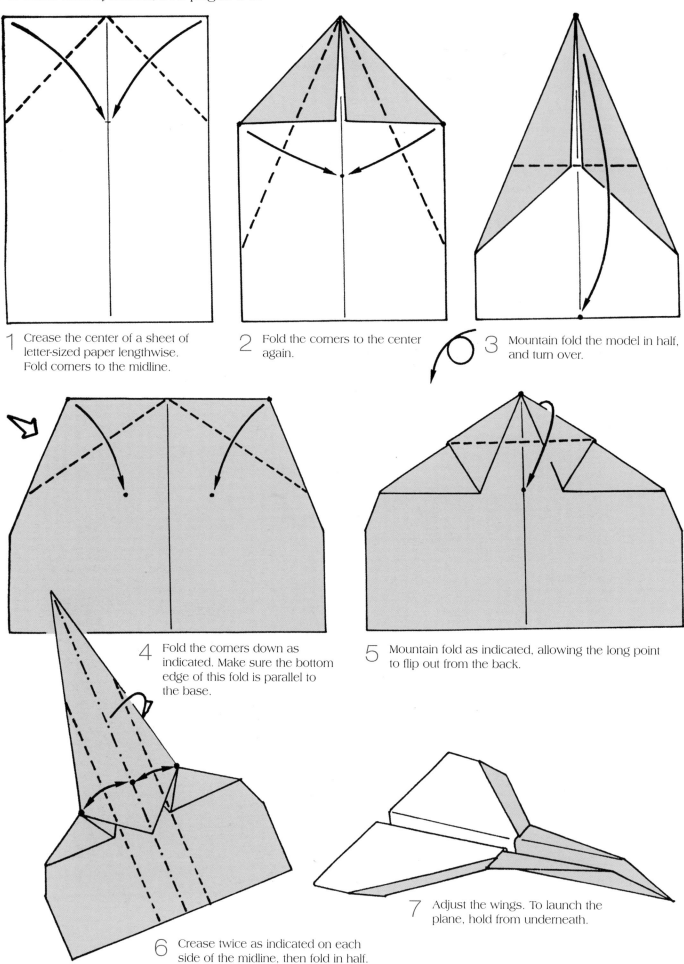

1 Crease the center of a sheet of letter-sized paper lengthwise. Fold corners to the midline.

2 Fold the corners to the center again.

3 Mountain fold the model in half, and turn over.

4 Fold the corners down as indicated. Make sure the bottom edge of this fold is parallel to the base.

5 Mountain fold as indicated, allowing the long point to flip out from the back.

6 Crease twice as indicated on each side of the midline, then fold in half.

7 Adjust the wings. To launch the plane, hold from underneath.

Uranus Arc II

WINNING PERFORMANCE. This plane won a competition at the Paris Air and Space Museum. Nicolas Beaudiez created the model, carefully balancing the front end and the wings. The plane should be launched from a high point.

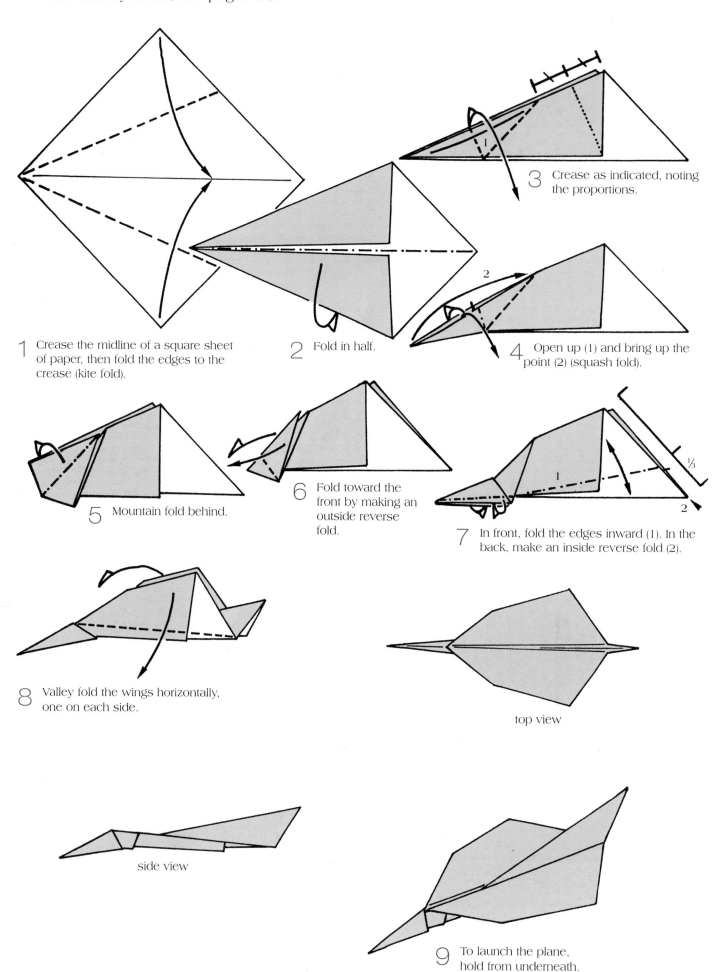

1 Crease the midline of a square sheet of paper, then fold the edges to the crease (kite fold).

2 Fold in half.

3 Crease as indicated, noting the proportions.

4 Open up (1) and bring up the point (2) (squash fold).

5 Mountain fold behind.

6 Fold toward the front by making an outside reverse fold.

7 In front, fold the edges inward (1). In the back, make an inside reverse fold (2).

8 Valley fold the wings horizontally, one on each side.

top view

side view

9 To launch the plane, hold from underneath.

Air Show

FIGHTER PLANE. This fold comes to us directly from Japan. Its creator, Eiki Momotani, won an international competition for its design.

For folds and symbols, see pages 5-9.

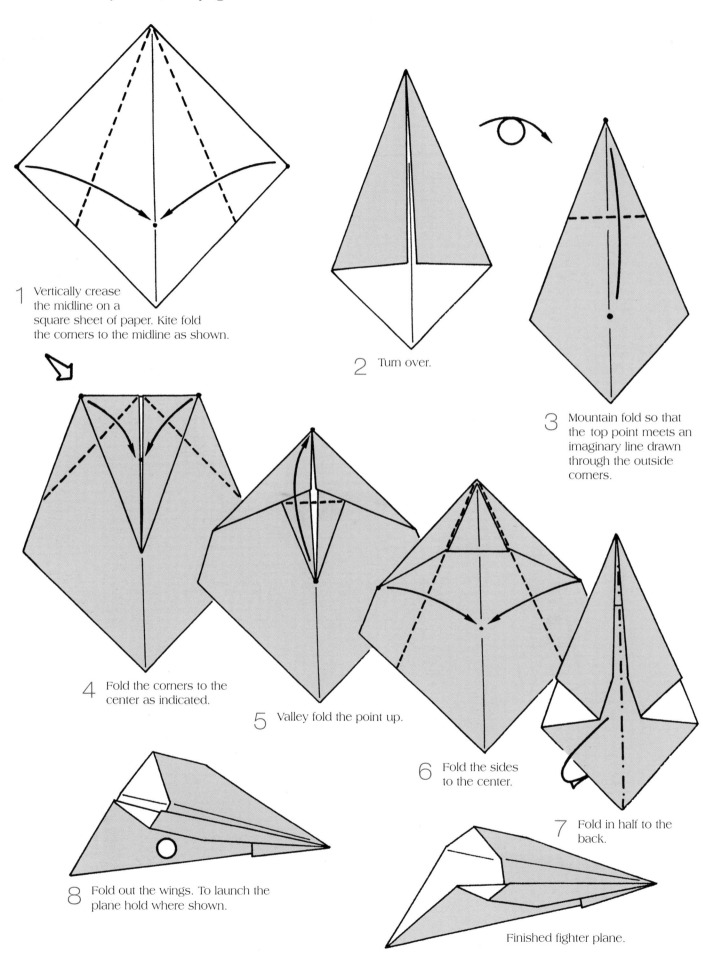

1 Vertically crease the midline on a square sheet of paper. Kite fold the corners to the midline as shown.

2 Turn over.

3 Mountain fold so that the top point meets an imaginary line drawn through the outside corners.

4 Fold the corners to the center as indicated.

5 Valley fold the point up.

6 Fold the sides to the center.

7 Fold in half to the back.

8 Fold out the wings. To launch the plane hold where shown.

Finished fighter plane.

No Stopovers

ROUND TRIP. This model, created by the Japanese origamist Takeshi Inoué, is actually a boomerang plane. Launch it, and it returns in a wide loop. Try catching the plane in the palm of your hand without letting it touch the ground.

For folds and symbols, see pages 5-9.

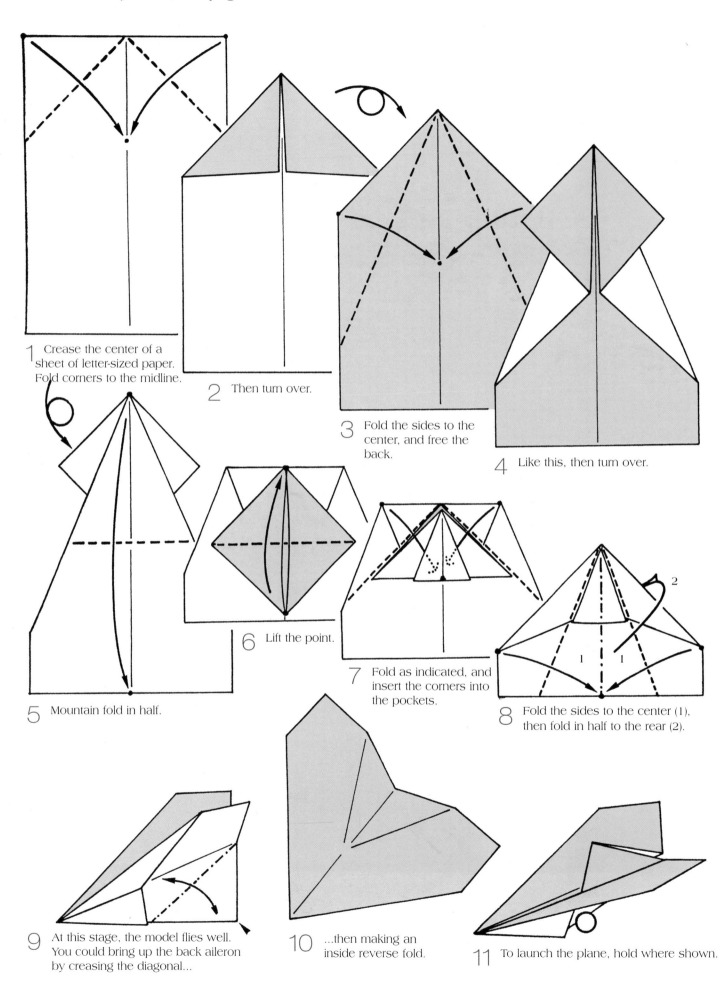

1 Crease the center of a sheet of letter-sized paper. Fold corners to the midline.

2 Then turn over.

3 Fold the sides to the center, and free the back.

4 Like this, then turn over.

5 Mountain fold in half.

6 Lift the point.

7 Fold as indicated, and insert the corners into the pockets.

8 Fold the sides to the center (1), then fold in half to the rear (2).

9 At this stage, the model flies well. You could bring up the back aileron by creasing the diagonal...

10 ...then making an inside reverse fold.

11 To launch the plane, hold where shown.

Glider 2

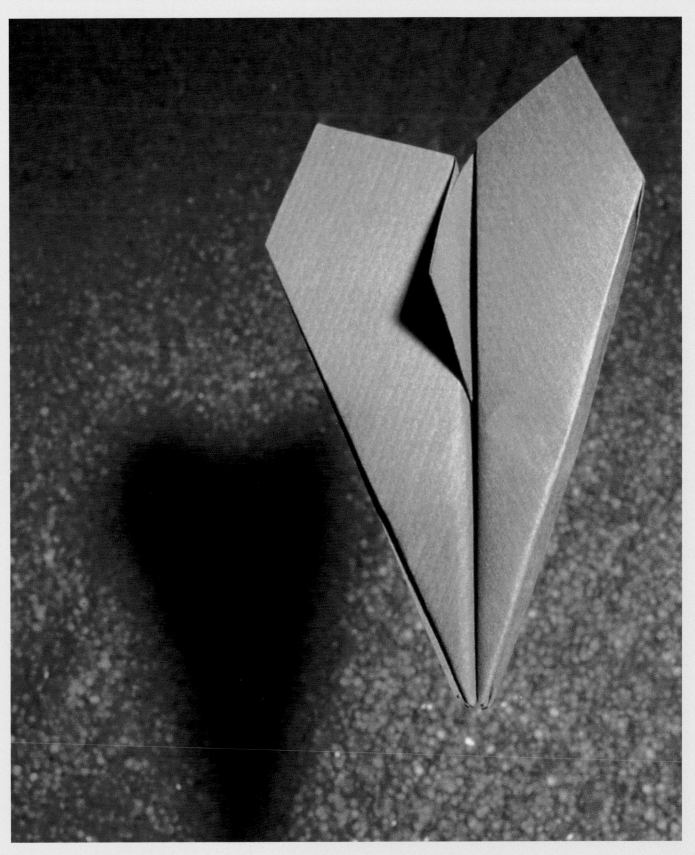

LONG-DISTANCE FLYER. Try to use an A4 sheet, since this fold takes advantage of the perfect proportions of that page size. (An 8½ x 11 sheet will work, though not quite as well.) The plane is heavy enough to be flown outdoors.

For folds and symbols, see pages 5-9.

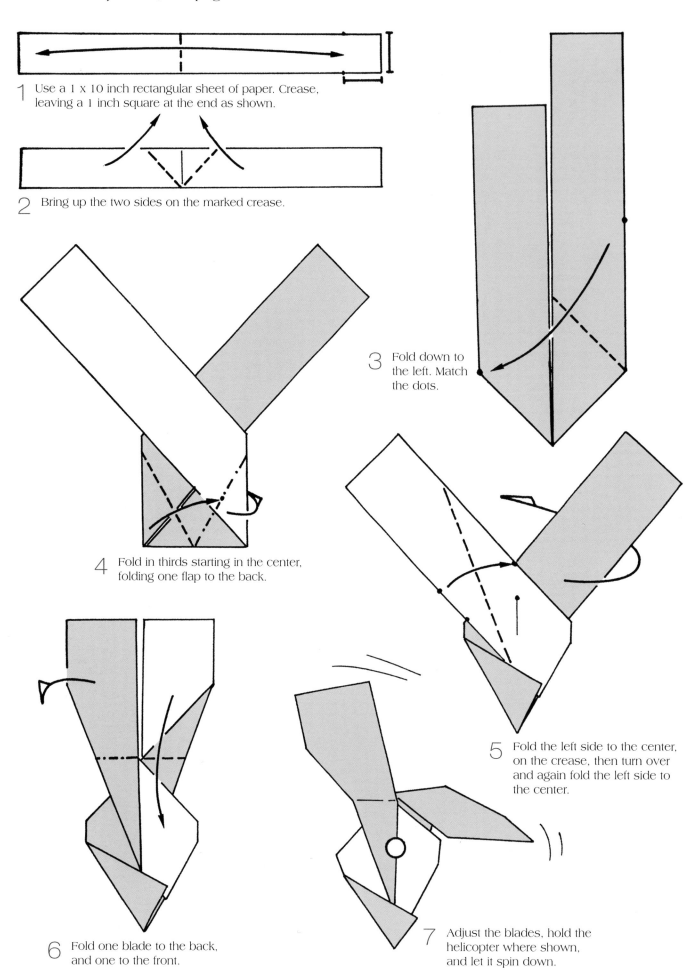

1 Use a 1 x 10 inch rectangular sheet of paper. Crease, leaving a 1 inch square at the end as shown.

2 Bring up the two sides on the marked crease.

3 Fold down to the left. Match the dots.

4 Fold in thirds starting in the center, folding one flap to the back.

5 Fold the left side to the center, on the crease, then turn over and again fold the left side to the center.

6 Fold one blade to the back, and one to the front.

7 Adjust the blades, hold the helicopter where shown, and let it spin down.

Helicopter

SPIRALING. During stopovers, the French pilot and author Antoine de Saint-Exupéry loved to fold helicopters like this one. Then he would send them into the air, to the delight of children. This model is based on the author's original fold.

For folds and symbols, see pages 5-9.

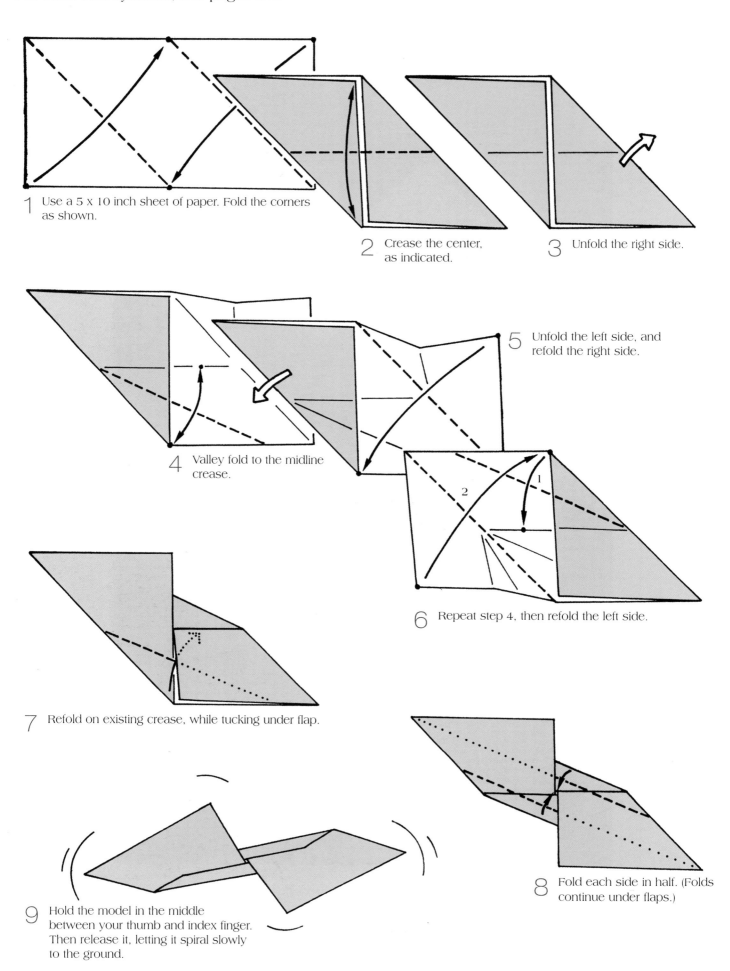

1 Use a 5 x 10 inch sheet of paper. Fold the corners as shown.

2 Crease the center, as indicated.

3 Unfold the right side.

4 Valley fold to the midline crease.

5 Unfold the left side, and refold the right side.

6 Repeat step 4, then refold the left side.

7 Refold on existing crease, while tucking under flap.

8 Fold each side in half. (Folds continue under flaps.)

9 Hold the model in the middle between your thumb and index finger. Then release it, letting it spiral slowly to the ground.

Rotor

EITHER WAY. This twin-blade model will fly in either direction, depending on how the first folds were made. That's why it's called ROTOR. Read forward or backward, the name is the same.

Animals

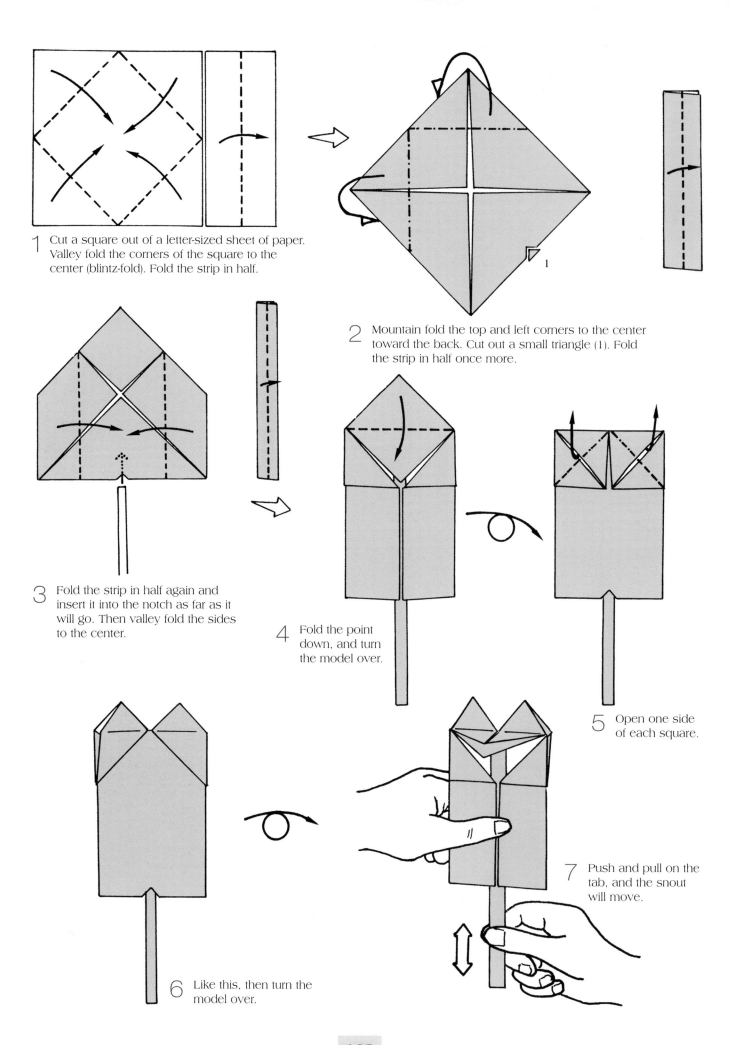

1 Cut a square out of a letter-sized sheet of paper. Valley fold the corners of the square to the center (blintz-fold). Fold the strip in half.

2 Mountain fold the top and left corners to the center toward the back. Cut out a small triangle (1). Fold the strip in half once more.

3 Fold the strip in half again and insert it into the notch as far as it will go. Then valley fold the sides to the center.

4 Fold the point down, and turn the model over.

5 Open one side of each square.

6 Like this, then turn the model over.

7 Push and pull on the tab, and the snout will move.

Chatty Fox

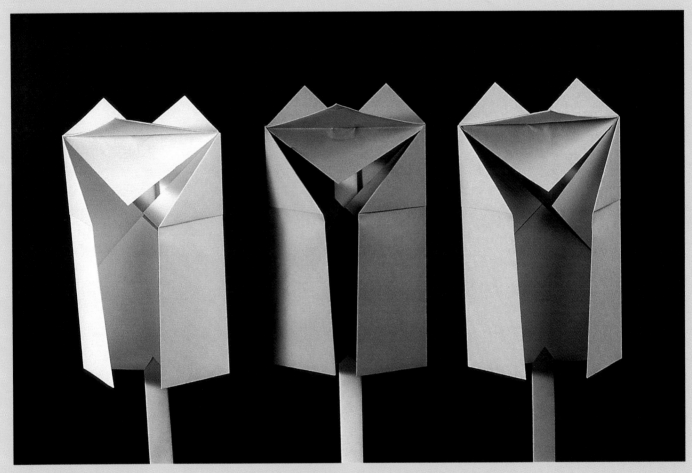

FROM HAND TO HAND. We don't know the precise origin of this delightful fold. Discovered by a Parisian schoolboy, it seems, the fox eventually became an established member of the paper-fold repertoire.

For folds and symbols, see pages 5-9.

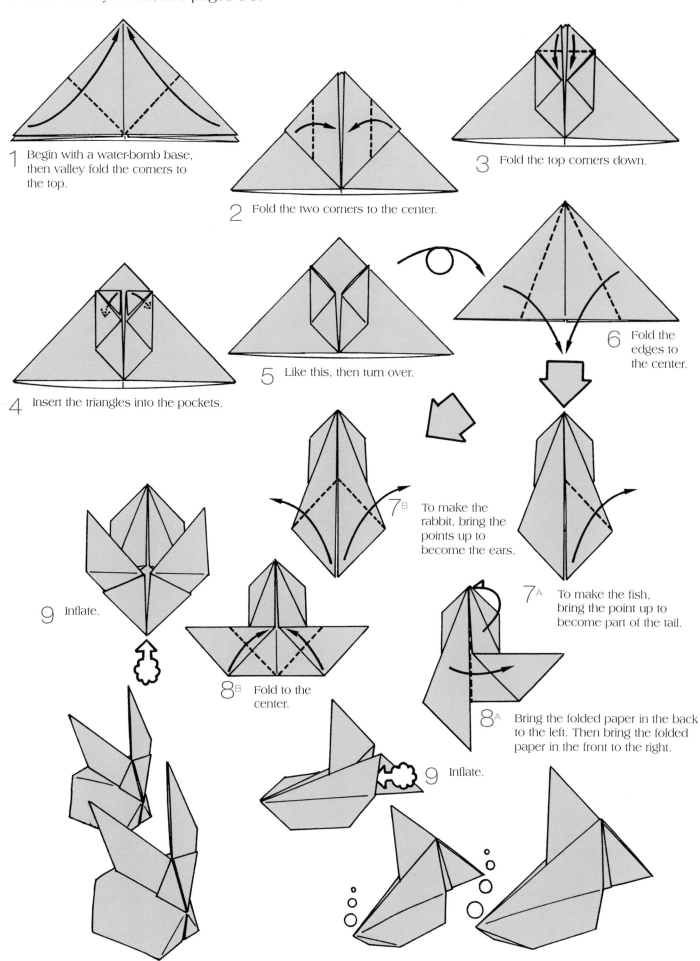

1 Begin with a water-bomb base, then valley fold the corners to the top.

2 Fold the two corners to the center.

3 Fold the top corners down.

4 Insert the triangles into the pockets.

5 Like this, then turn over.

6 Fold the edges to the center.

7B To make the rabbit, bring the points up to become the ears.

7A To make the fish, bring the point up to become part of the tail.

8B Fold to the center.

8A Bring the folded paper in the back to the left. Then bring the folded paper in the front to the right.

9 Inflate.

9 Inflate.

Fish and Rabbit

SWIM OR HOP. These two models are based on one of the oldest folding constructions, the water bomb. You can use either fold as a candy box or a container for holding little surprises.

For folds and symbols, see pages 5-9.

Body

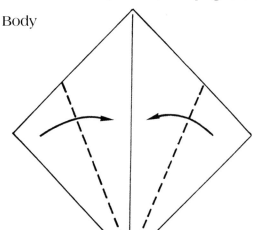

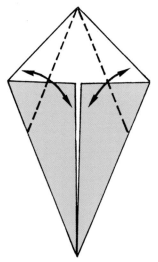

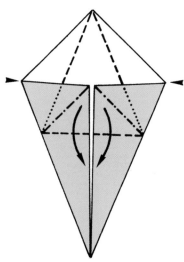

1 Crease the diagonal of a square sheet of paper as shown. Then fold the edges to the center.

2 Then crease the points to the center.

3 Fold the inner corners down, paying close attention to the direction of the creases.

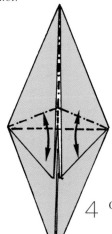

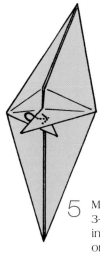

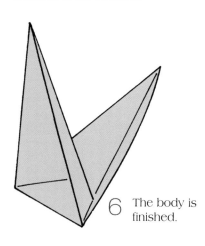

4 Crease as indicated.

5 Make the model 3-dimensional by inserting the tabs one into the other.

6 The body is finished.

Head

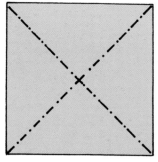

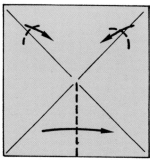

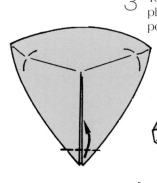

3 To lock step 2 in place, bring the point upward.

1 Use a square sheet of paper one-quarter the size of the body. Crease the diagonals.

2 Curve the upper corners, and give the model dimension by folding the lower triangle in half.

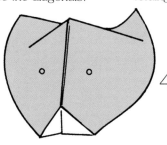

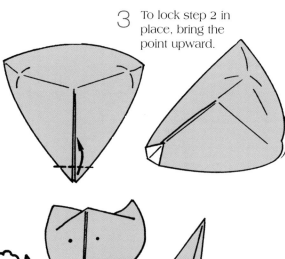

4 The head is finished.

Balance the head on the point of the body. The puppy will nod his head at the slightest movement of air.

Puppy

HAPPY POOCH. This little fellow is constructed of two pieces. At the slightest breeze he'll nod his head in contentment.

For folds and symbols, see pages 5-9.

Beak 1

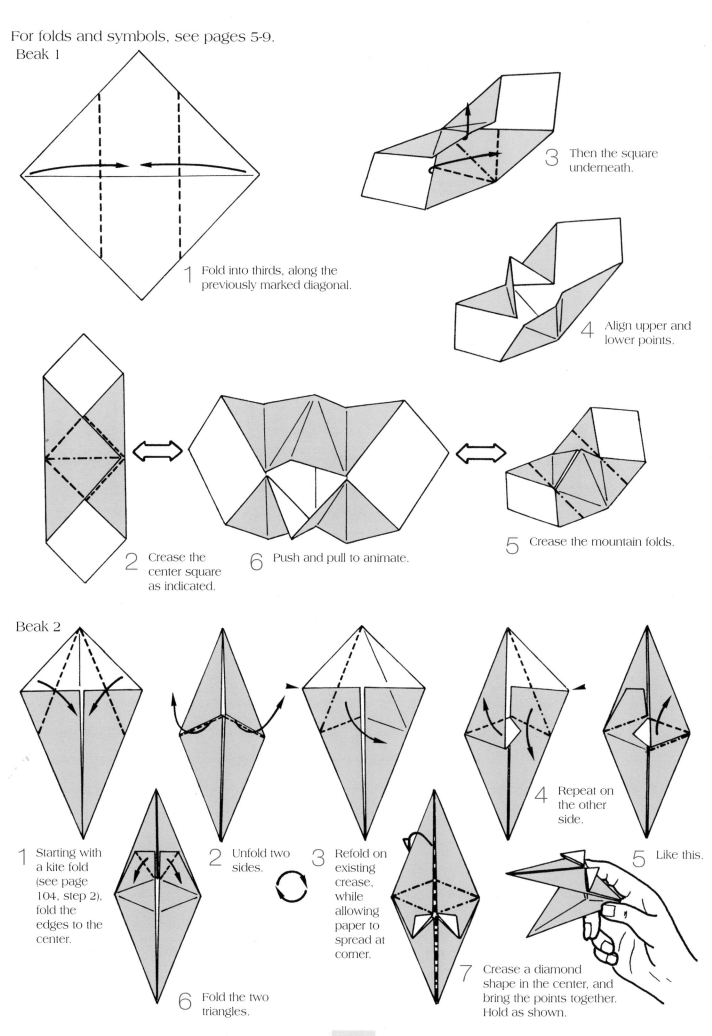

1 Fold into thirds, along the previously marked diagonal.

2 Crease the center square as indicated.

3 Then the square underneath.

4 Align upper and lower points.

5 Crease the mountain folds.

6 Push and pull to animate.

Beak 2

1 Starting with a kite fold (see page 104, step 2), fold the edges to the center.

2 Unfold two sides.

3 Refold on existing crease, while allowing paper to spread at corner.

4 Repeat on the other side.

5 Like this.

6 Fold the two triangles.

7 Crease a diamond shape in the center, and bring the points together. Hold as shown.

Talking Beaks

BARNYARD CHATTER. These two beaks are fairly easy to
fold. Keep them handy...between the pages of a book, or in
your pocket. They're always ready for a chat or a laugh.

Frog 1

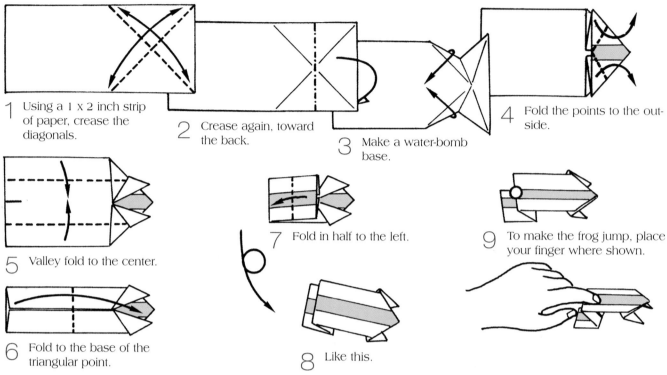

1 Using a 1 x 2 inch strip of paper, crease the diagonals.

2 Crease again, toward the back.

3 Make a water-bomb base.

4 Fold the points to the outside.

5 Valley fold to the center.

6 Fold to the base of the triangular point.

7 Fold in half to the left.

8 Like this.

9 To make the frog jump, place your finger where shown.

Frog 2

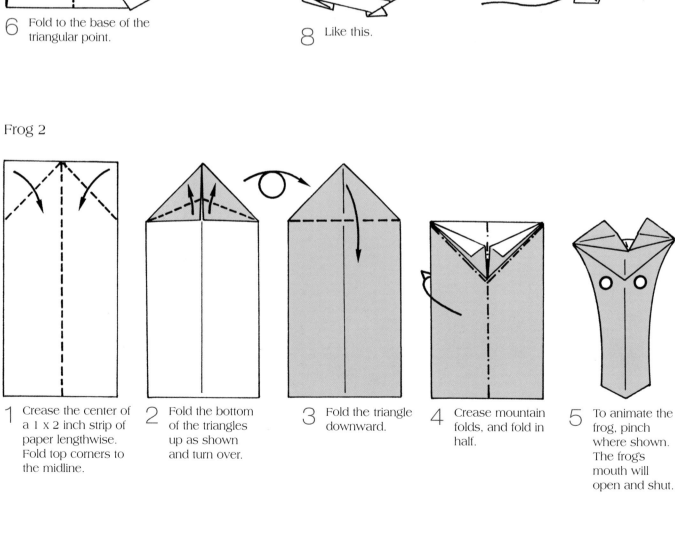

1 Crease the center of a 1 x 2 inch strip of paper lengthwise. Fold top corners to the midline.

2 Fold the bottom of the triangles up as shown and turn over.

3 Fold the triangle downward.

4 Crease mountain folds, and fold in half.

5 To animate the frog, pinch where shown. The frog's mouth will open and shut.

Frogs

LEAPING AND LIVELY. The first frog will run through an obstacle course or do long or high jumps. The second one is less athletic, but chattier. It comes to life when you hold it between thumb and index finger, exerting slight pressure.

For folds and symbols, see pages 5-9.

Bird

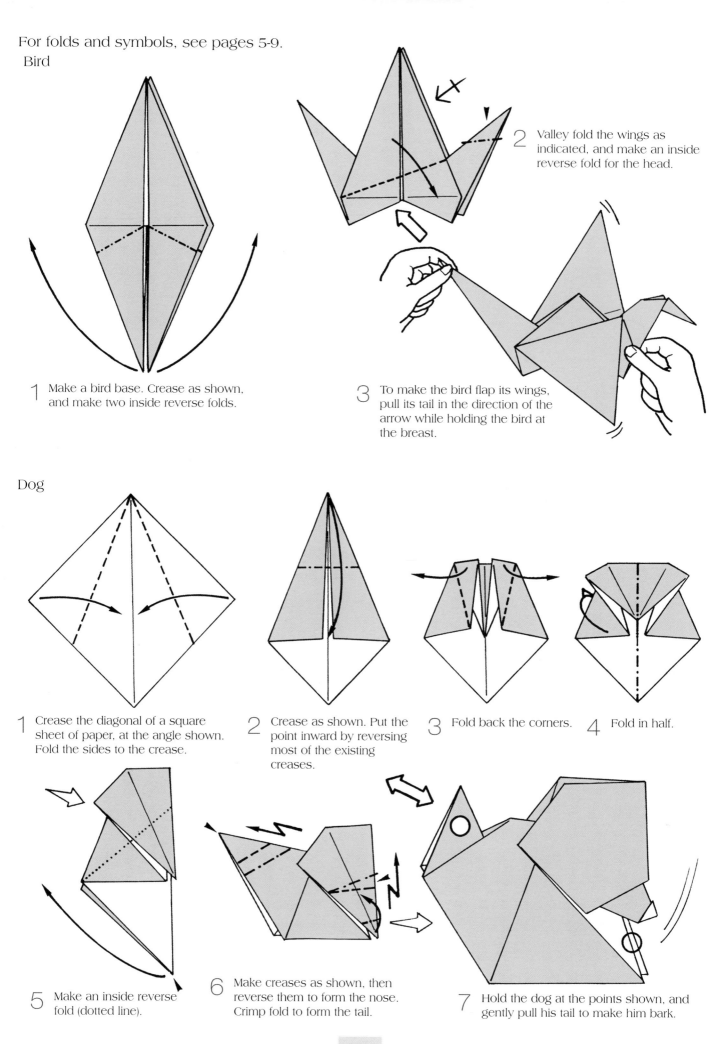

1 Make a bird base. Crease as shown, and make two inside reverse folds.

2 Valley fold the wings as indicated, and make an inside reverse fold for the head.

3 To make the bird flap its wings, pull its tail in the direction of the arrow while holding the bird at the breast.

Dog

1 Crease the diagonal of a square sheet of paper, at the angle shown. Fold the sides to the crease.

2 Crease as shown. Put the point inward by reversing most of the existing creases.

3 Fold back the corners.

4 Fold in half.

5 Make an inside reverse fold (dotted line).

6 Make creases as shown, then reverse them to form the nose. Crimp fold to form the tail.

7 Hold the dog at the points shown, and gently pull his tail to make him bark.

Bird

Dog

GRACEFUL. This traditional folding is among the oldest and best known origami models. After World War II, the Japanese made the crane a symbol of peace.

PLAYFUL. The dog is just waiting to lift his nose and start barking. Just hold him as shown, gently tweaking his little tail.

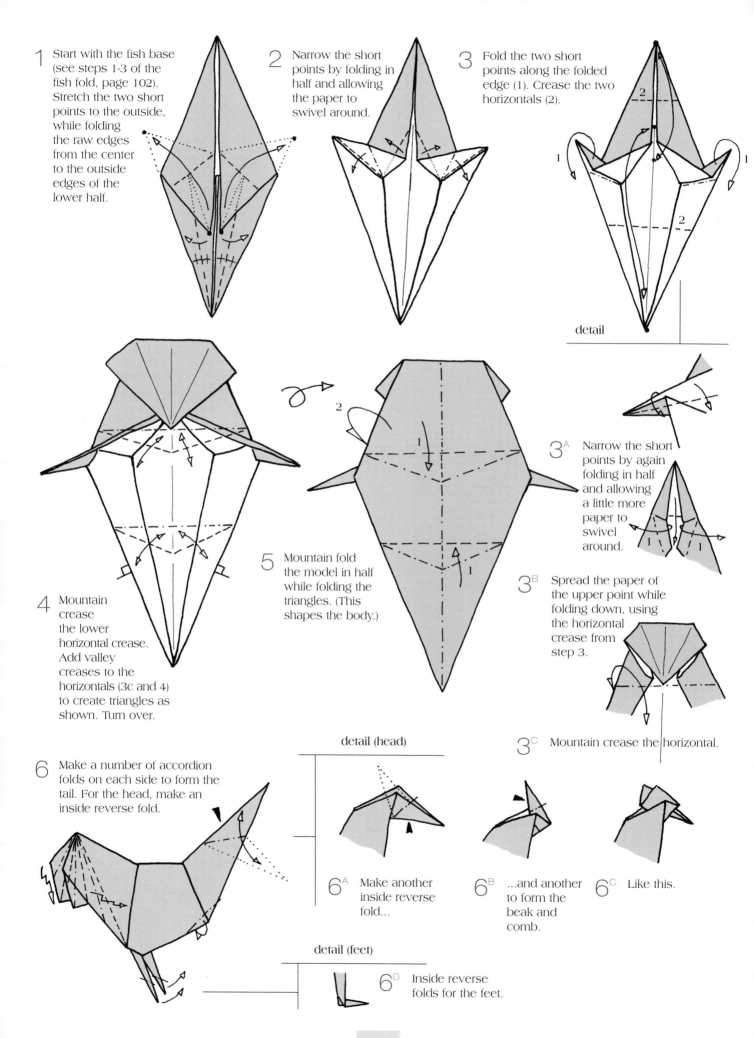

1 Start with the fish base (see steps 1-3 of the fish fold, page 102). Stretch the two short points to the outside, while folding the raw edges from the center to the outside edges of the lower half.

2 Narrow the short points by folding in half and allowing the paper to swivel around.

3 Fold the two short points along the folded edge (1). Crease the two horizontals (2).

detail

3ᴬ Narrow the short points by again folding in half and allowing a little more paper to swivel around.

3ᴮ Spread the paper of the upper point while folding down, using the horizontal crease from step 3.

3ᶜ Mountain crease the horizontal.

4 Mountain crease the lower horizontal crease. Add valley creases to the horizontals (3c and 4) to create triangles as shown. Turn over.

5 Mountain fold the model in half while folding the triangles. (This shapes the body.)

detail (head)

6ᴬ Make another inside reverse fold...

6ᴮ ...and another to form the beak and comb.

6ᶜ Like this.

6 Make a number of accordion folds on each side to form the tail. For the head, make an inside reverse fold.

detail (feet)

6ᴰ Inside reverse folds for the feet.

Pecking Hen

CHICKEN FEED. When they're not sitting on their eggs, the hens in the coop busily peck at grain and small insects. This model is for experienced folders.

For folds and symbols, see pages 5-9.

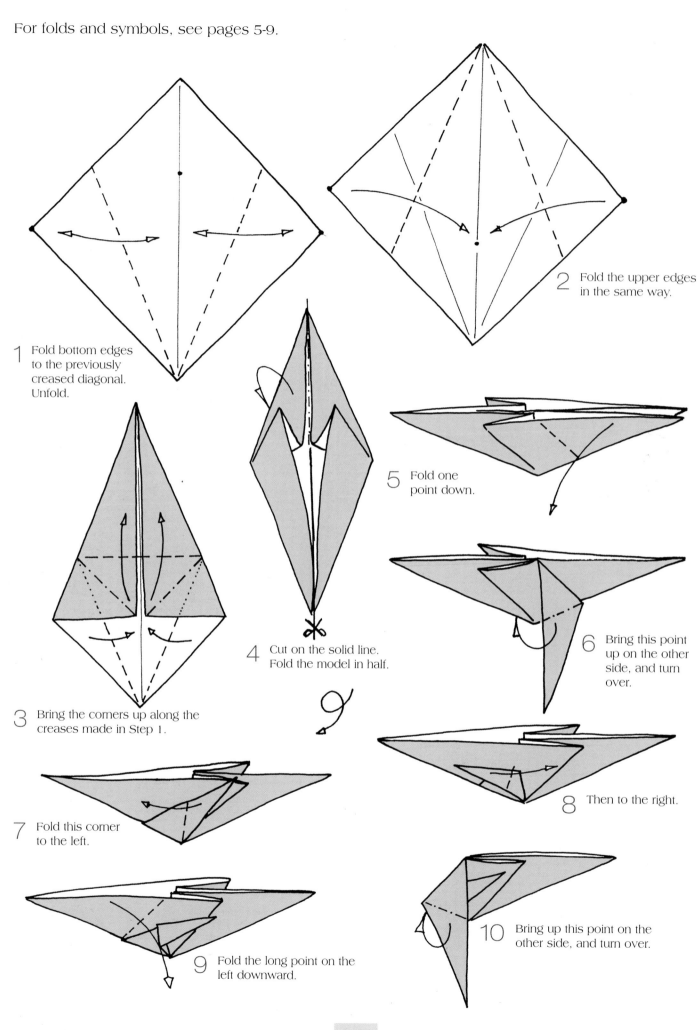

2 Fold the upper edges in the same way.

1 Fold bottom edges to the previously creased diagonal. Unfold.

5 Fold one point down.

3 Bring the corners up along the creases made in Step 1.

4 Cut on the solid line. Fold the model in half.

6 Bring this point up on the other side, and turn over.

7 Fold this corner to the left.

8 Then to the right.

9 Fold the long point on the left downward.

10 Bring up this point on the other side, and turn over.

Swimming Fish

SCHOOL OF FISH. By resting on three supporting points, these little swimmers give the illusion that they are moving with the current. This is a good fold for beginners.

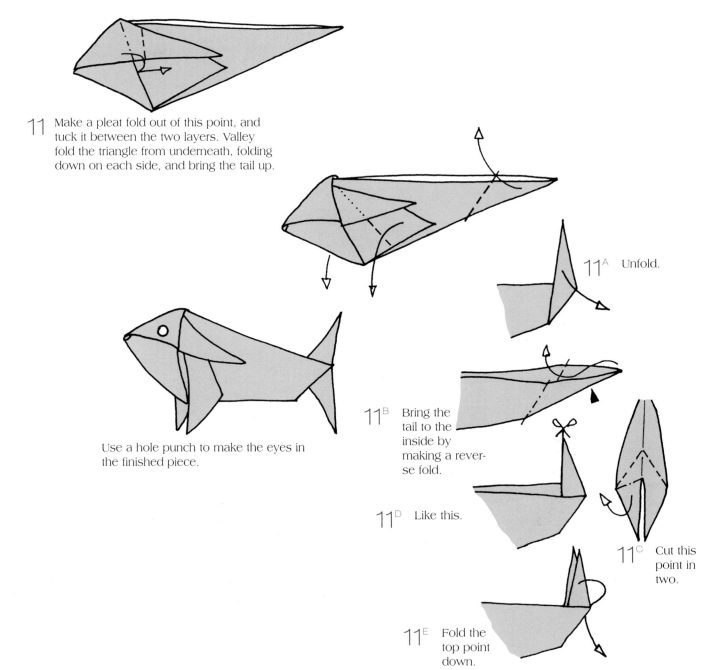

11 Make a pleat fold out of this point, and tuck it between the two layers. Valley fold the triangle from underneath, folding down on each side, and bring the tail up.

11^A   Unfold.

11^B   Bring the tail to the inside by making a reverse fold.

11^C   Cut this point in two.

11^D   Like this.

11^E   Fold the top point down.

Use a hole punch to make the eyes in the finished piece.

116

Owl

PLANNING AHEAD. Did you ever wonder how the owl sleeps without tumbling from his perch? Actually, he's usually resting, just getting ready to hunt in the moonlight.

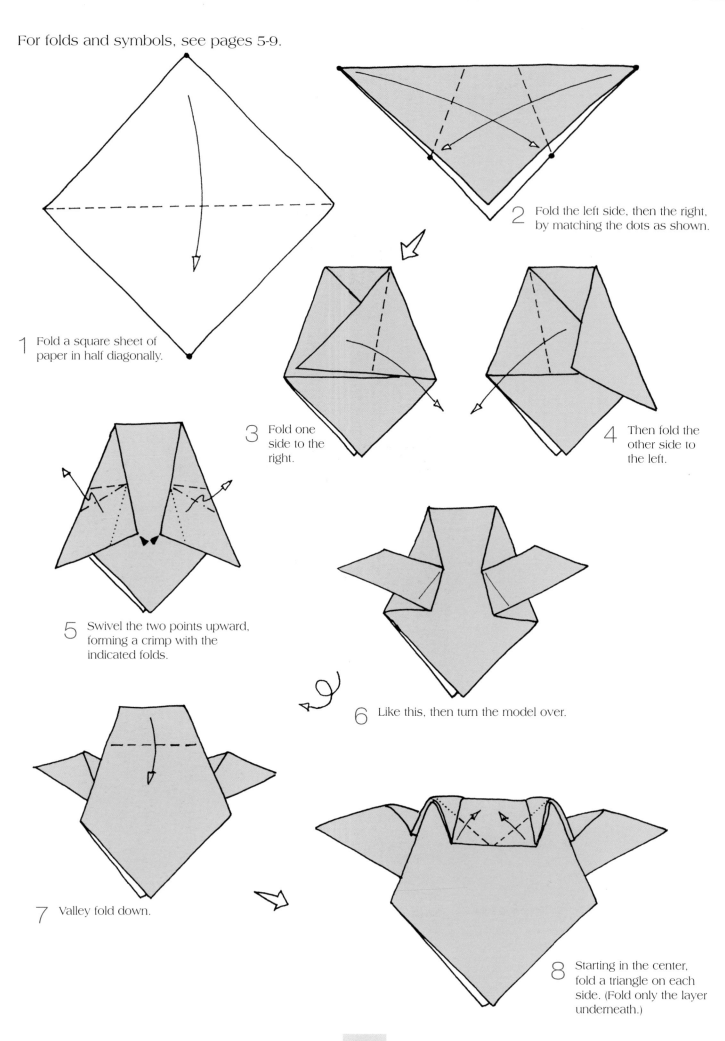

1 Fold a square sheet of paper in half diagonally.

2 Fold the left side, then the right, by matching the dots as shown.

3 Fold one side to the right.

4 Then fold the other side to the left.

5 Swivel the two points upward, forming a crimp with the indicated folds.

6 Like this, then turn the model over.

7 Valley fold down.

8 Starting in the center, fold a triangle on each side. (Fold only the layer underneath.)

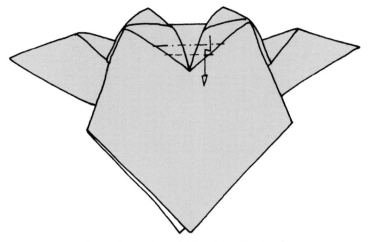

9 Make a pleat fold to form the beak.

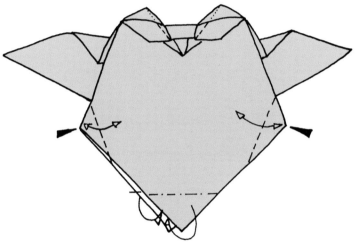

10 Make the eyes by inserting your fingertip into the two pockets above and to either side of the beak. Then sink the side and fold the bottom points inward.

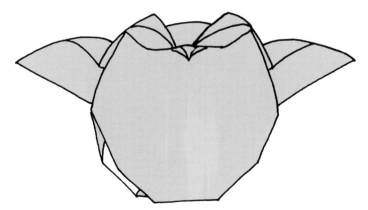

11 To make the owl stand upright, open the base slightly and curve its wings.

1 Mountain fold a square in half diagonally.

2 Fold the two sides upward on the diagonal as shown.

3 Fold the two sides upward once more.

4 Cut a very fine strip in all layers.

5 In each strip you will find another strip. Fold the inside strips forward as far as possible to make the antennae.

Grasshopper

LEAPS AND BOUNDS. Thanks to its strong and flexible hind legs, the grasshopper is an extraordinary jumper. Use thin paper and have fun folding this model.

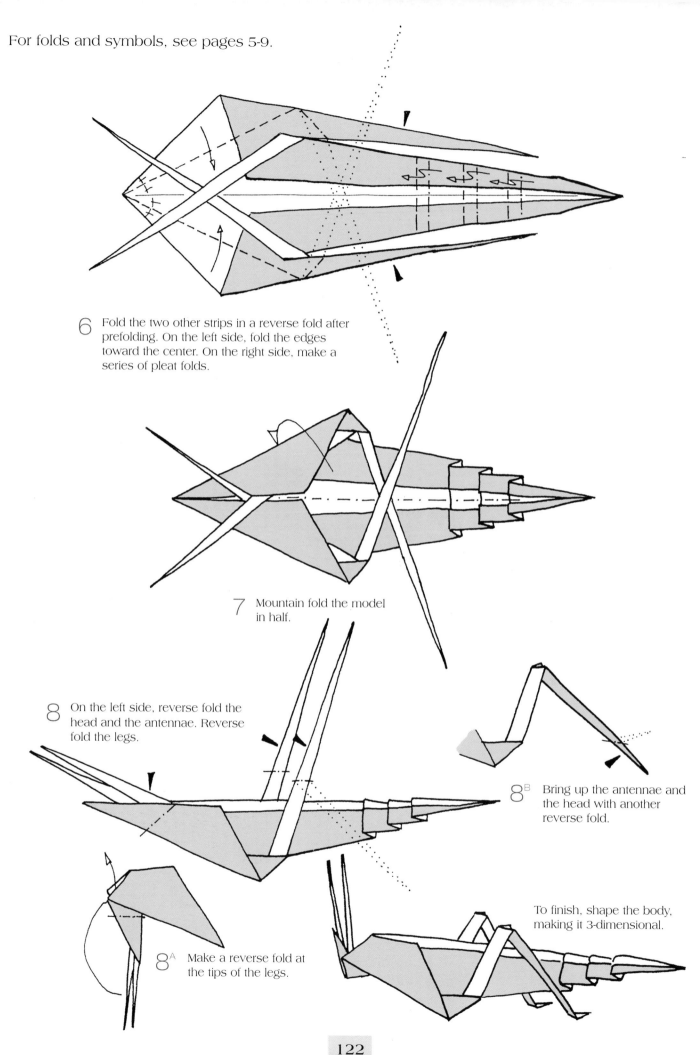

6 Fold the two other strips in a reverse fold after prefolding. On the left side, fold the edges toward the center. On the right side, make a series of pleat folds.

7 Mountain fold the model in half.

8 On the left side, reverse fold the head and the antennae. Reverse fold the legs.

8ᴮ Bring up the antennae and the head with another reverse fold.

8ᴬ Make a reverse fold at the tips of the legs.

To finish, shape the body, making it 3-dimensional.

Penguin

WADDLING ALONG. Standing up, this penguin resembles a little man in a tuxedo. He loves sliding on the ice and jumping feet first into the water. This fold is of medium difficulty.

For folds and symbols, see pages 5-9.

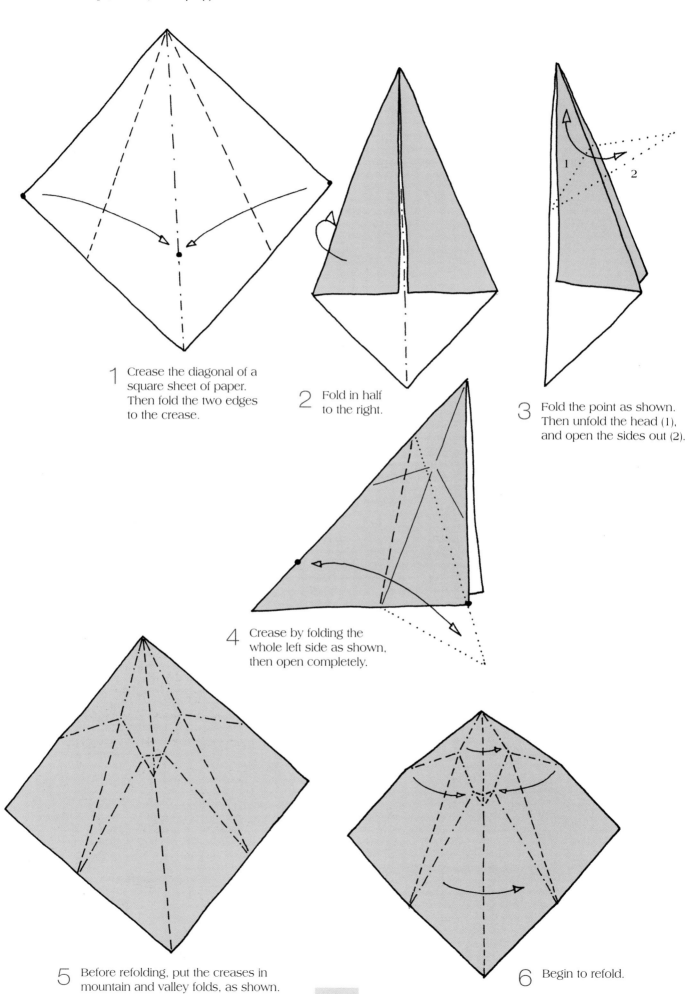

1 Crease the diagonal of a square sheet of paper. Then fold the two edges to the crease.

2 Fold in half to the right.

3 Fold the point as shown. Then unfold the head (1), and open the sides out (2).

4 Crease by folding the whole left side as shown, then open completely.

5 Before refolding, put the creases in mountain and valley folds, as shown.

6 Begin to refold.

124

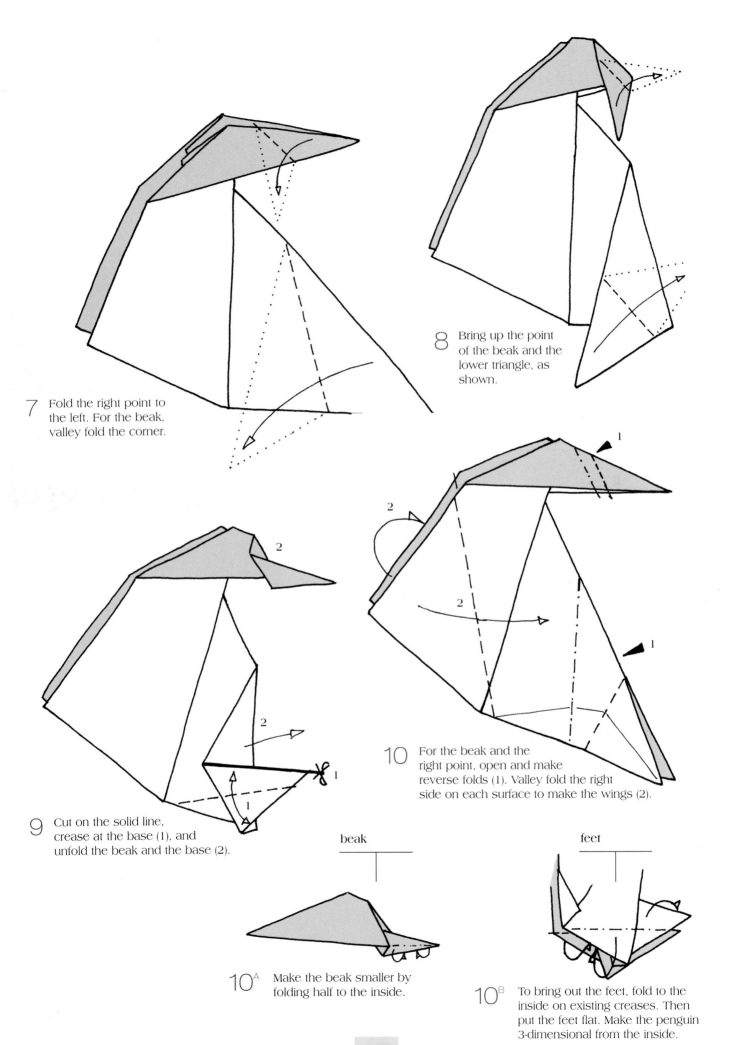

7 Fold the right point to the left. For the beak, valley fold the corner.

8 Bring up the point of the beak and the lower triangle, as shown.

9 Cut on the solid line, crease at the base (1), and unfold the beak and the base (2).

10 For the beak and the right point, open and make reverse folds (1). Valley fold the right side on each surface to make the wings (2).

beak

feet

10ᴬ Make the beak smaller by folding half to the inside.

10ᴮ To bring out the feet, fold to the inside on existing creases. Then put the feet flat. Make the penguin 3-dimensional from the inside.

The
magic folds

For folds and symbols, see pages 5-9.

1 Take a heavy sheet of paper, or a sheet of Bristol board, 2½ x 5 inches. Mark the midline crease using valley and mountain folds. Make accordion folds on both sides, approximately ½ inch wide as shown.

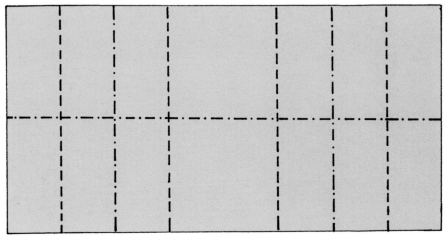

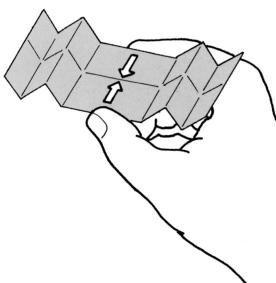

2 Take the card between your thumb and index finger as shown, and exert a slight pressure. The card will fold upon itself as if by magic.

Magic Card

ASTONISHING. This amazing fold was introduced to me by a renowned magician. With a slight pressure of the fingers, plus great concentration, you can get the card to fold upon itself as if by magic.

Finger Puppet

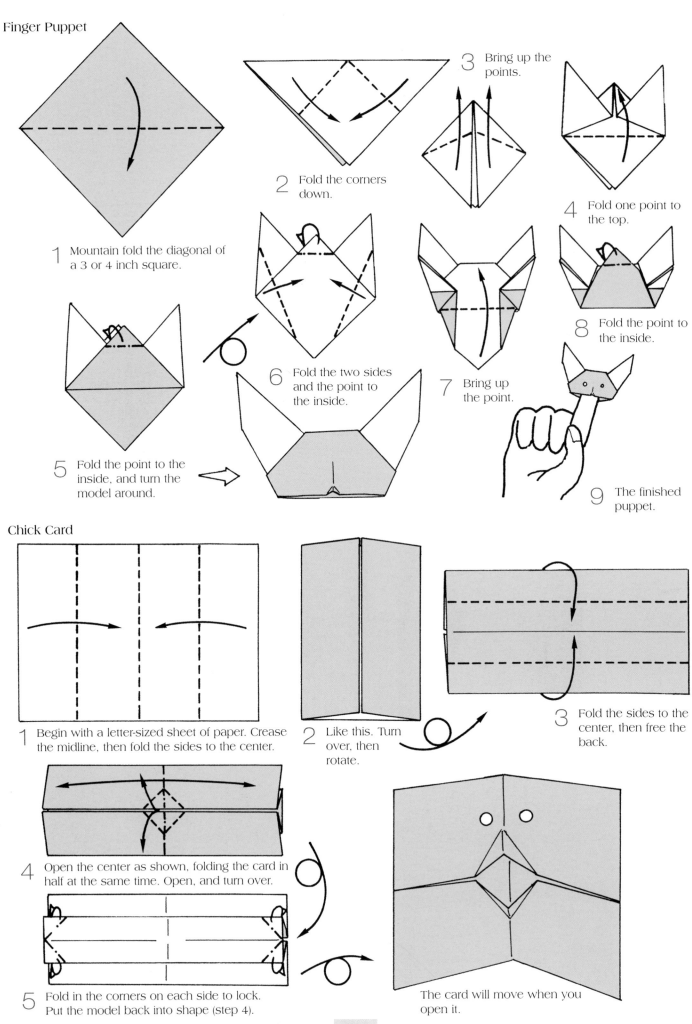

1 Mountain fold the diagonal of a 3 or 4 inch square.

2 Fold the corners down.

3 Bring up the points.

4 Fold one point to the top.

5 Fold the point to the inside, and turn the model around.

6 Fold the two sides and the point to the inside.

7 Bring up the point.

8 Fold the point to the inside.

9 The finished puppet.

Chick Card

1 Begin with a letter-sized sheet of paper. Crease the midline, then fold the sides to the center.

2 Like this. Turn over, then rotate.

3 Fold the sides to the center, then free the back.

4 Open the center as shown, folding the card in half at the same time. Open, and turn over.

5 Fold in the corners on each side to lock. Put the model back into shape (step 4).

The card will move when you open it.

Finger Puppet

TRADITIONAL. The little puppets come alive as soon as they sit on your fingertips. Two hands just don't seem to be enough.

Chick Card

SPONTANEOUS. This card can be sent on various occasions. Wish friends a happy anniversary with it, or use it to announce the arrival of a baby. Open the card. The chick is just waiting to sing a cheery message.

For folds and symbols, see pages 5-9.

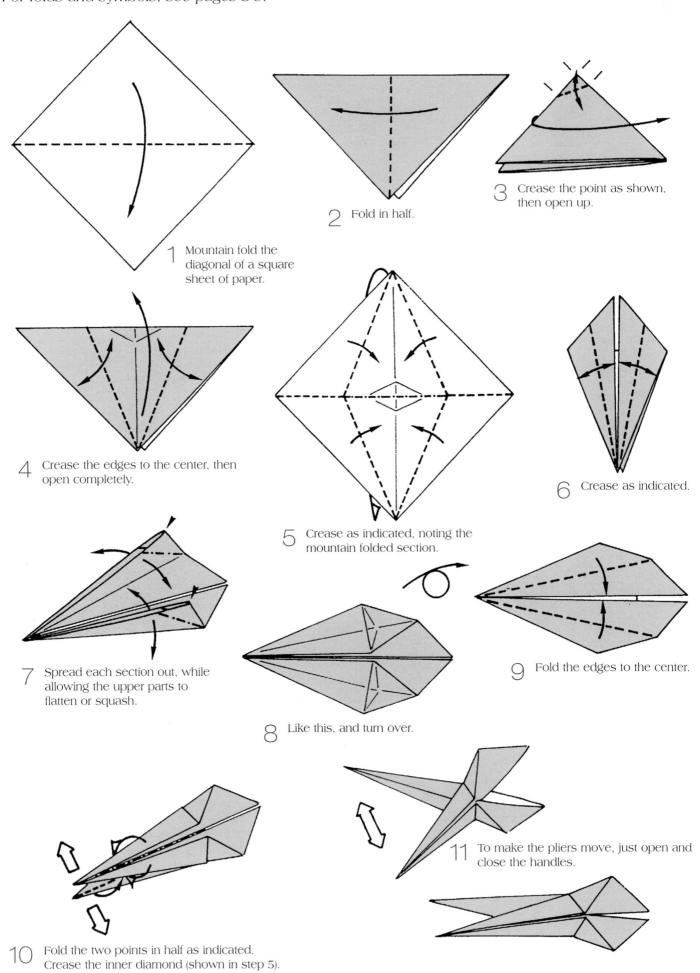

1 Mountain fold the diagonal of a square sheet of paper.

2 Fold in half.

3 Crease the point as shown, then open up.

4 Crease the edges to the center, then open completely.

5 Crease as indicated, noting the mountain folded section.

6 Crease as indicated.

7 Spread each section out, while allowing the upper parts to flatten or squash.

8 Like this, and turn over.

9 Fold the edges to the center.

10 Fold the two points in half as indicated. Crease the inner diamond (shown in step 5).

11 To make the pliers move, just open and close the handles.

Pliers

SAFETY ON THE JOB. If you're working on a project and your child wants to help, what could be nicer than the two of you folding a pair of pliers? These paper pliers open and close when you move the handles.

For folds and symbols, see pages 5-9.

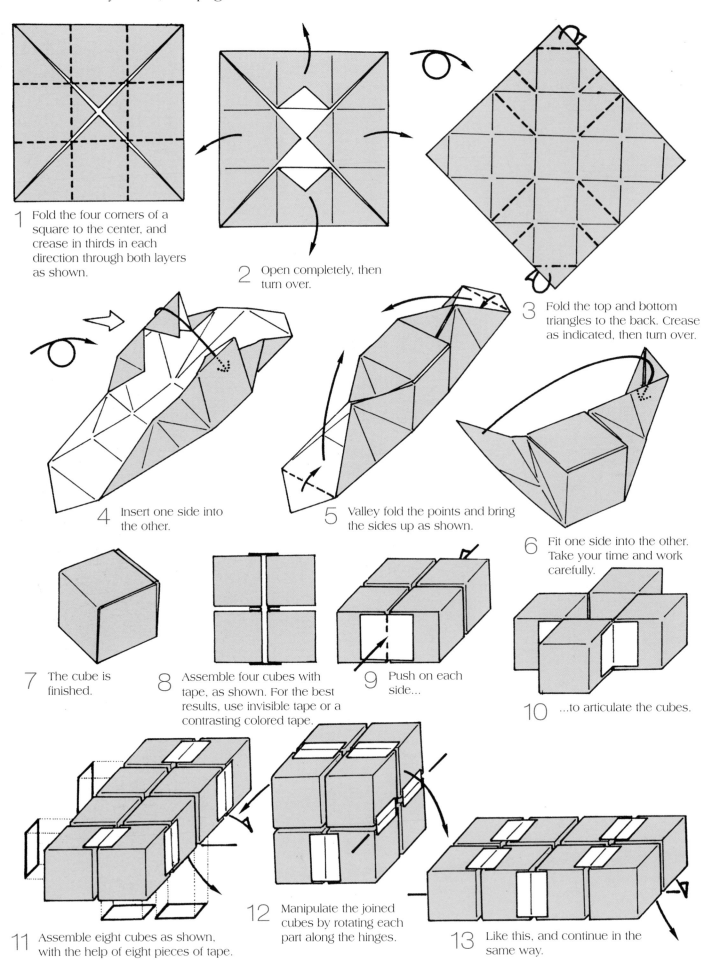

1 Fold the four corners of a square to the center, and crease in thirds in each direction through both layers as shown.

2 Open completely, then turn over.

3 Fold the top and bottom triangles to the back. Crease as indicated, then turn over.

4 Insert one side into the other.

5 Valley fold the points and bring the sides up as shown.

6 Fit one side into the other. Take your time and work carefully.

7 The cube is finished.

8 Assemble four cubes with tape, as shown. For the best results, use invisible tape or a contrasting colored tape.

9 Push on each side...

10 ...to articulate the cubes.

11 Assemble eight cubes as shown, with the help of eight pieces of tape.

12 Manipulate the joined cubes by rotating each part along the hinges.

13 Like this, and continue in the same way.

Hinged Cubes

NEW ARRANGEMENTS. To create these two models, you first fold the cubes. Then you assemble in fours, using a little tape. A bit of manipulation, and you can transform any design you've drawn on the surfaces. Assembling the cubes in eights is more difficult, but the results are quite amazing. The very ambitious folder can assemble twelve cubes.

For folds and symbols, see pages 5-9.

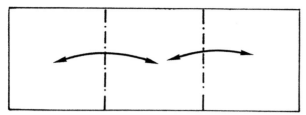

1 Mountain fold a large rectangular sheet of paper (with a three-to-one ratio) into thirds, as indicated.

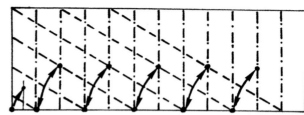

2 Divide each of the three parts with four vertical creases. Join the marked dots (starting at the left), creating diagonal valley folds. Pay close attention to the spacing.

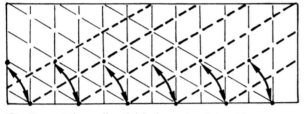

3 Repeat the valley folds from the right side.

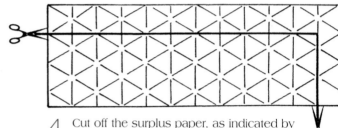

4 Cut off the surplus paper, as indicated by the solid lines.

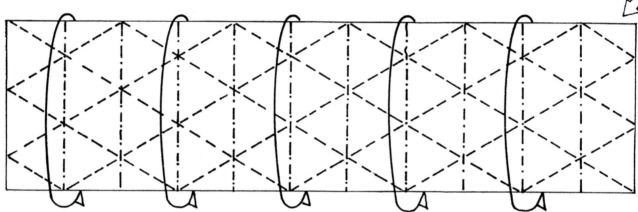

5 Roll the strip upon itself, respecting the direction of the folds.

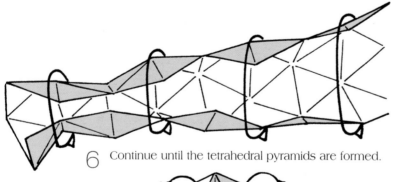

6 Continue until the tetrahedral pyramids are formed.

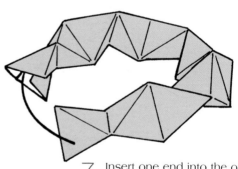

7 Insert one end into the other, as shown.

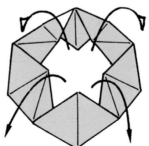

8 The closed chain turns upon itself...

9 ...infinitely.

Tetrahedral Chain

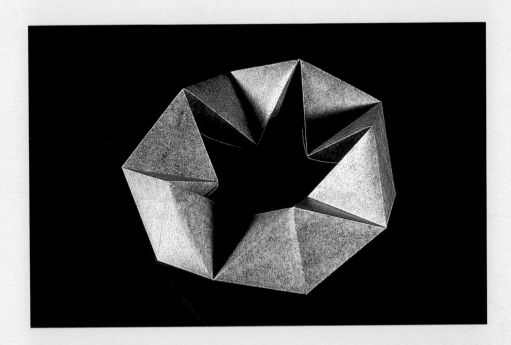

INFINITY. Because this project demands meticulous attention to so many details, it is best suited for highly experienced folders. Once finished the chain will turn upon itself smoothly, like the gears of a well-oiled machine.

For folds and symbols, see pages 5-9.

Moving Lever

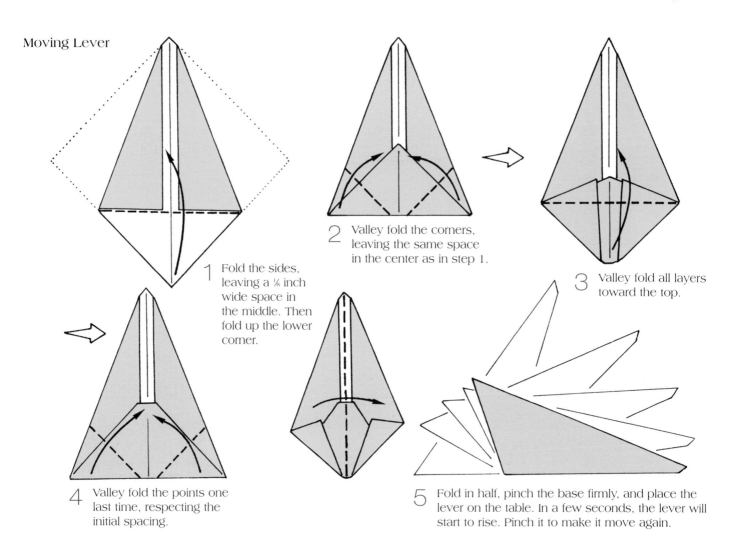

1 Fold the sides, leaving a ⅛ inch wide space in the middle. Then fold up the lower corner.

2 Valley fold the corners, leaving the same space in the center as in step 1.

3 Valley fold all layers toward the top.

4 Valley fold the points one last time, respecting the initial spacing.

5 Fold in half, pinch the base firmly, and place the lever on the table. In a few seconds, the lever will start to rise. Pinch it to make it move again.

Circle to Square

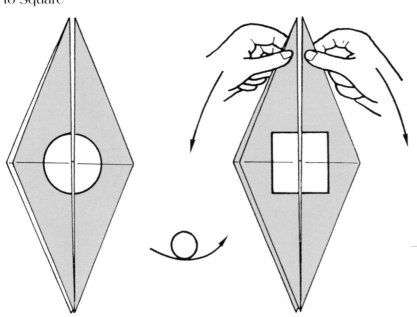
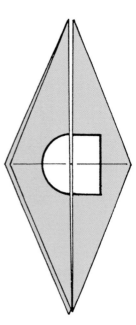

1 Start by folding a bird base. Draw a circle, fold down the top layer, and turn the model over.

2 Draw a square on this side. To combine the two figures, fold one point toward the top.

3 A new figure appears.

Moving Lever

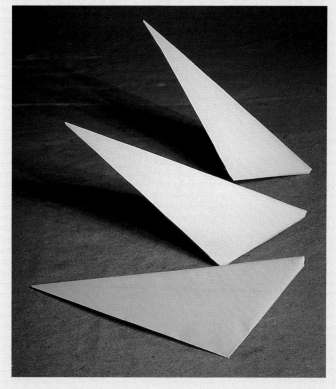

UPWARDLY MOBILE. Who would believe that a folded paper square could become a lever that gradually rises. (You, of course, after a pinch or two.)

From Circle to Square

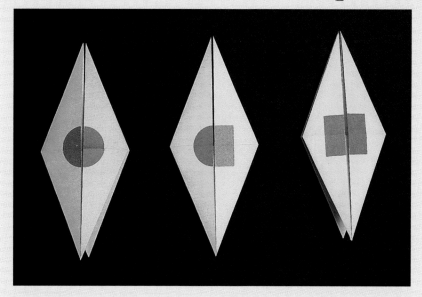

ILLUSIONS. This model is really nothing more than a bird base, on which you have drawn a circle on one side and a square on the other. Fold the points toward the bottom and the circle and the square combine to confuse you completely.

For folds and symbols, see pages 5-9.

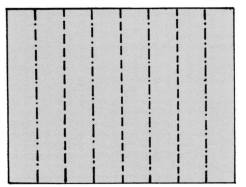

1 Divide a rectangular sheet of paper into eight equal parts and make accordion folds.

2 Crease through all layers in both directions, bisecting the angle, as shown.

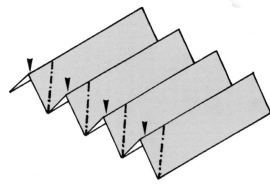

3 Make inside reverse folds.

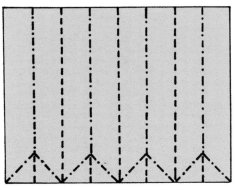

4 The fold gives this pattern. Tuck the triangle under and refold in accordion folds.

5 Crease a second fold in both directions.

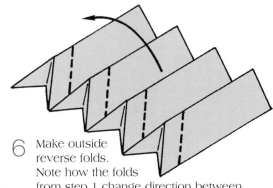

6 Make outside reverse folds. Note how the folds from step 1 change direction between successive reverse folds.

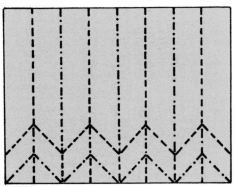

7 Observe the direction of the folds, and place the whole model down flat.

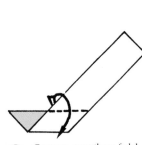

8 Crease another fold.

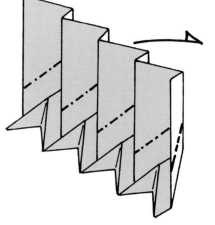

9 Proceed in the same way.

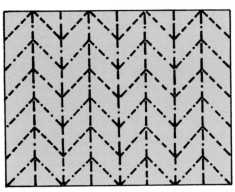

10 Repeat the herringbone patterns until you run out of paper.

11 To make the pattern move, just pull and push at opposite corners.

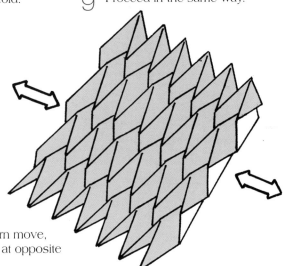

Herringbone

AGILE FINGERS. This model requires tremendous dexterity, and is best left to the experienced folder. It's a purely decorative fold that catches the light through a play of shadows.

For folds and symbols, see pages 5-9.

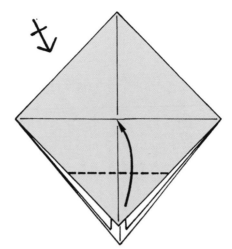

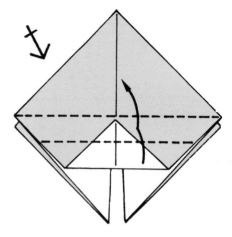

1   On a square sheet of paper, make a preliminary base and crease a diagonal. Repeat behind.

2   Fold the point to the center on the crease. Repeat behind.

3   Roll up by folding on the crease. Repeat behind.

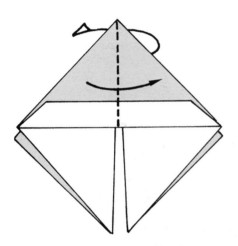

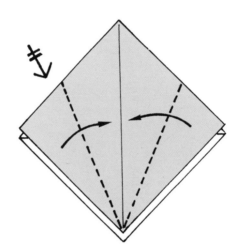

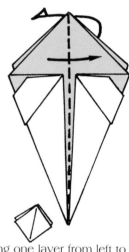

4   Fold one layer from the left to right. Repeat behind.

5   Fold the sides to the center. Repeat behind.

6   Bring one layer from left to right. Repeat behind.

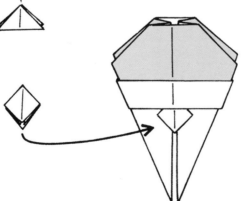

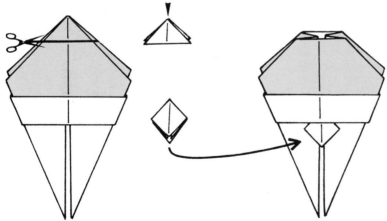

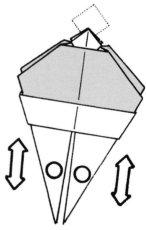

7   Cut off the point. Invert the piece you cut off by pressing on the middle.

8   Slide this preliminary mini-base between the points.

9   When you pull the two points back and forth, the little creature climbs up and reappears through the hole at the top.

The Little Creature that Climbs

REAPPEARING ACT. This amazing fold comes to us from England by way of Mauritius and France. Watch this clever creature disappear, then continue on its path and reappear through the hole at the top.

Appendix

Before you begin, read through the section on Folds and Symbols (pages 5-9), which explains the essential folds and symbols used throughout this book.

How to Fold

Each step of folding is represented by an arrow or by dots that are paired up. To avoid errors, make sure you understand the difference between "folding" the paper and "creasing" the fold. In the first instance, you keep the fold. In the second, you fold as indicated by the double arrow and then unfold; you leave the crease for the next step. If necessary, refer to the next step to help you understand the one you are working on.

Which Paper to Use

Practice folding using the suggested paper size, and begin by choosing simple models using ordinary paper. Get to know your paper by folding and handling it. Is its texture silky or grainy? Is its surface shiny or matte? How transparent is it? Use your fingertips to get an idea of its thickness. How well does it hold its creases? You may want to know where the paper comes from.

The best type of paper should weigh no more than about 4 ounces. Origami paper, or Pop'set or Kraft, will work well.

How to Cut Your Paper

Paper that comes in large sheets should be cut in squares. Use an X-acto knife, scissors, or a guillotine-style cutter. You can easily cut squares from 8½ x 11 paper. Just draw a right angle first.

Levels of Difficulty

The table of contents codes the level of difficulty for each model: one star for the easiest folds, three for the most difficult.

Always feel free to follow your imagination, adding a personal touch to the original.